T0370174

Day Hike!
MOUNT RAINIER

5th Edition

Day Hike!

WASHINGTON

MOUNT RAINIER

5th Edition

**More than 50 Trails around Mount Rainier
National Park, Longmire, and Paradise Area**

———————————

Ron C. Judd

SASQUATCH BOOKS
SEATTLE

Copyright © 2002, 2009, 2014, 2019, 2025 by Ron C. Judd and Seabury Blair Jr.

Printed in China

Sasquatch Books with colophon is a registered trademark of Blue Star Press, LLC

29 28 27 26 25   9 8 7 6 5 4 3 2 1

Editorial: Meri-Jo Borzilleri | Cover photograph: © Don Landwehrle/Adobe Stock |
Cover design: Hillary Grant and Tony Ong | Interior design: Andrew Fuller and
Tony Ong | Interior photographs: Ron C. Judd and Seabury Blair Jr. | Page 186:
Additional photo by Robynn Rockstad (Tolmie Peak Lookout) | Maps: Marlene Blair

Library of Congress Cataloging-in-Publication Data is available

ISBN: 978-1-63217-552-6

IMPORTANT NOTE: Please use common sense. No guidebook can act as a substitute for
experience, careful planning, the right equipment, and appropriate training. There is
inherent danger in all the activities described in this book, and readers must assume full
responsibility for their own actions and safety. Changing or unfavorable conditions in
weather, roads, trails, snow, waterways, and so forth cannot be anticipated by the author
or publisher, but should be considered by any outdoor participants. The author and
publisher will not be responsible for the safety of users of this guide, and neither of
them shall be liable or responsible for any legal liability, or any loss or damage or
physical injury of any kind, allegedly arising from any information herein.

   Given the potential for changes to trail accessibility and hiking rules and regulations
post-publication, please check ahead for updates on contact information, parking
passes, and camping permits.

Sasquatch Books | 1325 Fourth Avenue, Suite 1025 | Seattle, WA 98101
SasquatchBooks.com

CONTENTS

Carbon Glacier/ Mowich Lake, 165

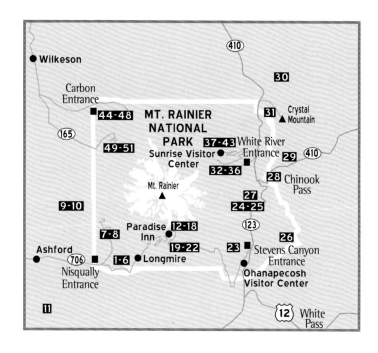

HIKES AT A GLANCE

Easy

NO.	HIKE NAME	RATING	TRAIL ACCESSIBLE	KIDS	DOGS	♿
1.	Kautz Creek	★ ★ ★	June–Nov	✔		
2.	Twin Firs Loop	★ ★ ★	Year-round	✔		
3.	Trail of the Shadows	★ ★ ★	Year-round	✔		✔
5.	Carter/Madcap Falls	★ ★ ★	July–Oct	✔		
7.	Round Pass	★ ★ ★ ★	Year-round	✔		✔
9.	Goat Lake	★ ★ ★ ★	June–Oct	✔	✔	
12.	Nisqually Vista	★ ★ ★ ★ ★	July–Oct	✔		✔
16.	Paradise to Narada Falls	★ ★ ★	Mid-June–Oct	✔		
24.	Grove of the Patriarchs	★ ★ ★ ★ ★	June–Oct	✔		
25.	Silver Falls Loop	★ ★ ★ ★	May–Oct	✔		
28.	Naches Peak Loop	★ ★ ★ ★ ★	July–Oct	✔	✔	
34.	Emmons Moraine	★ ★ ★ ★	July–Oct	✔		
36.	Silver Forest/Emmons Vista	★ ★ ★	July–Oct	✔		
37.	Sunrise Rim Loop	★ ★ ★ ★	July–Oct	✔		
38.	Sourdough Ridge/Dege Peak	★ ★ ★	July–Oct	✔		

Moderate

NO.	HIKE NAME	RATING	TRAIL ACCESSIBLE	KIDS	DOGS	♿
4.	Rampart Ridge Loop	★ ★	June–Oct	✔		
8.	Lake George	★ ★ ★	June–Oct	✔		
10.	Glacier View	★ ★ ★ ★	July–Oct	✔	✔	
17.	Upper Paradise Valley	★ ★ ★ ★	Late June–Oct	✔		
18.	Paradise Glacier	★ ★ ★ ★	July–mid-Oct	✔		
19.	High Lakes Loop	★ ★ ★ ★	Late June–Oct	✔		
21.	Bench and Snow Lakes	★ ★ ★	July–Oct	✔		
27.	Eastside Trail	★ ★ ★	June–Nov	✔		
32.	Owyhigh Lakes	★ ★ ★ ★	July–Oct	✔		
33.	Summerland	★ ★ ★ ★ ★	July–Oct	✔		
34.	Glacier Basin	★ ★ ★ ★	July–Oct			
39.	Huckleberry Creek/Forest Lake	★ ★	Mid-July–Oct	✔		

NO.	HIKE NAME	RATING	TRAIL ACCESSIBLE	KIDS	DOGS	♿
40.	Frozen Lake/Mount Fremont Lookout	★★★★	July–Oct	✔		
42.	Berkeley Park	★★★	July–Oct	✔		
43.	Skyscraper Pass	★★★	Mid-July–Oct	✔		
44.	Green Lake	★★★	July–Oct	✔		✔
46.	Carbon Glacier Viewpoint	★★★★	July–Oct	✔		
51.	Spray Park	★★★★★	Mid-July–Oct	✔		

Moderately Difficult

NO.	HIKE NAME	RATING	TRAIL ACCESSIBLE	KIDS	DOGS	♿
6.	Comet Falls	★★★★	Mid-July–Oct	✔		
13.	Alta Vista	★★★★	July–Oct	✔		
20.	Pinnacle Saddle	★★★★	Mid-July–Oct	✔		
22.	Stevens Creek	★★	June–Oct			
29.	Sheep Lake	★★★	July–Oct	✔	✔	
30.	Noble Knob	★★★★	July–Oct	✔	✔	
31.	Crystal Lakes	★★★★	July–Oct	✔		
35.	Palisades Lakes	★★★	July–Oct			
41.	Burroughs Mountain	★★★★★	Late July–late Oct			
49.	Mowich River Camp	★★★★	July–Oct	✔		

Difficult

NO.	HIKE NAME	RATING	TRAIL ACCESSIBLE	KIDS	DOGS	♿
1.	Indian Henry's Hunting Ground	★★★	June–Nov			
6.	Van Trump Park	★★★★	Mid-July–Oct			
11.	High Rock Lookout	★★★	June–Oct	✔	✔	
14.	Panorama Point/Skyline Loop	★★★★★	Late July–mid-Oct			✔
23.	Cowlitz Divide	★★★★	July–Oct			
26.	Three Lakes	★★★★	July–Oct			
45.	Really Big Tree/Ipsut Pass	★★	July–Oct	✔		
47.	Cataract Camp/Seattle Park	★★	July–Oct			
48.	Yellowstone Cliffs	★	July–Oct			
50.	Tolmie Peak/Eunice Lake	★★★	July–Oct			

Extreme

NO.	HIKE NAME	RATING	TRAIL ACCESSIBLE	KIDS	DOGS	♿
15.	Camp Muir	★★★★	Mid-July–Sept			

ACKNOWLEDGMENTS

The fifth edition of this guide is dedicated to the memory of Lou Whittaker, legendary mountaineer and iconic citizen of the Northwest, who died on March 24, 2024 at the age of 95. Whittaker, the twin brother of another climbing legend, Jim Whittaker, stood atop the mountain we honor here more than 250 times, and established and ran Rainier Mountaineering Inc., a pioneering commercial guide service, for more than half a century along with family members. His memory will live long on The Mountain.

—Ron C. Judd

MOUNT RAINIER (TAHOMA)

The more crazed the lowlands become, the more serene our high places seem.

In the bursting-at-the-seams Puget Sound region, nowhere is this more plainly evident than at Mount Rainier (also known by its Anglicized Indigenous name, Tahoma), the 14,411-foot, ice-crowned behemoth, which, it's easy to imagine, often looks down at the increasingly urbanized steel-and-glass jungle of the Seattle area and furrows its glaciated brow. Or perhaps even rolls its summit-crater eyes.

The decade and a half that has passed since the first edition of this guide has seen seismic shifts in the way of life of the average Northwest resident. The once-sleepy city of Seattle, long exuding a laid-back nature that belied its size, has undergone a sweeping transformation with formerly quiet neighborhoods radically altered by construction projects spurred by a tech-fueled economic boom. Population in the city and in its broad suburbs has also boomed. The entire pace, feel, and sensibility of the region has shifted in a manner no less than startling to residents with some degree of moss growing on the north slopes of their rooflines—and hairlines.

Traffic throughout the region, responding accordingly, has done the seemingly impossible by getting even slower. Getting out of the city or suburbs and into true wilderness, long the natural calling card of the Seattle area, is not as simple as it once was. And even when accomplished, it often means "sharing solitude"—if there can be such a thing—with more and more people.

As the fifth edition of this guide is completed in spring 2024, the ramifications of all those changes have spiked off the chart, in two tangible ways, both concerning.

One is that The Mountain whose icy countenance has always been there to cool our hot human flashes of anxiety is undeniably undergoing radical change. That's nothing new for a volcano, but what is new, and disturbing, is the cause: rapid melting of major Rainier glaciers in an era of accelerating climate change. Short-term impacts on access to portions of the mountain loom as giant question marks. But they literally ensure changes likely are coming.

The second is that overwhelming numbers of park visitors—with an initial surge likely spurred by the Covid pandemic charging along unabated—prompted the National Park Service in spring 2024 to move with uncharacteristic speed to do something that a half-century ago would have seemed unthinkable: Citing visitor numbers soaring from 1.1 million in 2013 to 2.5 million (in 1.1 million cars) by 2023, the park has implemented daily visitor limits at park entrance gates. These are already in effect; your next trip to Rainier is going to require even more planning. In the short term, that will require an entrance reservation, online or by phone, from May 24 through Labor Day. (You can read about the park's new permit entry system under "Permits/Contact," page xxiii.)

This is a lot to ponder, in a short amount of time. But for both veteran park visitors and rank newcomers, rest assured we can confirm the wonders of Mount Rainier are still wondrous in every way. The bit of extra effort to plan how and when to best enjoy them is worth it in every sense. And the limits on sheer numbers of visitors, we predict, are likely to benefit both park facilities and trails, and the user-experience of those inside the park on any given day.

With a little effort, tranquility still can be experienced at Mount Rainier National Park and other protected wilderness areas throughout the Northwest. The park, it is safe to say, will never revert to the Rainier of our youth. But, despite the increasingly chaotic region in which it sits and the ever-ascending visitation figures posted at its entrances, it remains a fortress of solitude for many of us. And every trip out over the fence of Western Washington's new normalcy and into the sunshine of the sweet alpine haunts of Rainier seems just that much sweeter.

Longstanding Northwestern contrasts, in other words, have been drawn in much sharper relief. Whether the response to that reality is despair or exultation is really up to each of us. A lot of us continue to choose the latter, celebrating the fact that even at this Northwest icon— inarguably one of America's most- beloved natural places— wild encounters can still be readily had by doing two stunningly simple things: donning a decent pair of boots and setting forth.

OK, it's not quite *that* simple. The determined seeker of wild solitude at the peak will need a bagful of essentials (including, we hope, the collected wisdom of resources such as this guide) to take full advantage of what Rainier offers. Even in the new cacophony that can feel like an 80-pound, ill-fitting backpack on our shoulders, setting out on a trail on the highlands or lowlands of Mount Rainier still leaves most of the teeming masses behind, and can seem every bit as magical as it once was. Perhaps more so.

'Twas always the case. As we have said here before: to truly *know* Rainier beyond its postcard image is to leave its congested parking lots and enter its wild spots, shake hands with its evergreens, breathe its crisp air, smell its wildflowers, and soak your aching feet in its cool streams.

These are all things, fortunately, that can be done easily, without venturing very far down any one of Mount Rainier National Park's 240 magical miles of maintained trails.

We emphasize here the word "easily." One of the great misperceptions of the mountain is that you have to be in Everest shape to partake of its 228,000 acres of pristine wilderness. This is understandable: just *look* at the thing. The mountain is huge, forbidding, and rough-hewn. Since Rainier truly is an exposed vertical being, much of its land is very rugged, and the terrain from its shoulders on up requires the kind of backcountry know-how you can't get by walking around Seattle's Green Lake a half-dozen times a year.

But all around this mountain's waistline, magic awaits. Alpine meadows too beautiful to be real. Sprawling snowfields; stunning views. Old-growth trees, bigger than your house. Liquid-crystal rivers. Box canyons. Two dozen of the most massive glaciers on the continent. Ample wildlife.

You can see some of it without ever getting 50 feet from your car. But you can't really see it until you're in it, and the best—and only—way to get there at Mount Rainier is by foot, down a path.

That's a simple lesson we learned anew by researching this guide, which aims to bring to life 51 of the greatest walking paths in the Northwest, if not the nation, for Rainier visitors who get to the mountain once a week or once in a lifetime.

They range from the awesome—and occasionally dangerous—alpine trek to Camp Muir above Paradise to a placid, universally overlooked path winding through old-growth forest west of Longmire. Most of the trails fall somewhere in between, and all of them remind us of a delightful fact often overshadowed by the mountain's sheer size: you can get out in Mount Rainier National Park—really out, in the memory-of-a-lifetime kind of way—without committing a week of your life or ten years' wear and tear on your knees.

Almost all the hikes listed in this guide can be undertaken by the average it's-a-sunny-Sunday-morning-let's-do-something-grand, sort-of hiker. Granted, some are steep, and hiking above 5,000 feet will leave the unconditioned flatlander huffing and puffing (take your time and hydrate; you'll adjust). Proper preparation and attention to weather, snow levels, and other factors are important. But the fact remains that Mount Rainier National Park presents a rare opportunity for both visitors and residents. Perhaps nowhere in the world is such a unique alpine environment within such close reach of a major metropolitan area.

This explains the crowds that plague the park on summer weekends—and threaten to make today's unfettered auto access to park attractions and trailheads a thing of the past. More than two million people visit the park each year, with the vast majority landing there on summer weekends.

Being park consumers in the same way you are, we've kept that in mind in preparing this guide, attempting to warn you away from the worst overcrowding—and suggesting alternatives to popular trails when there's simply no way you can get to the park except on that same sunny August weekend with everyone else.

One of the more profound findings in our summer-long trek through the park, however, was how easily solitude or near-solitude could be attained by walking more than a couple miles from some of Rainier's most overcrowded tourist haunts. Pick a trail from the guide, follow it as far as you will, and find out for yourself. You just might discover something about a place you thought you knew—and about yourself.

WHAT'S NEW IN THE FIFTH EDITION

With the second consecutive update inviting you to the wonders of Rainier in full color, the fifth edition is more user-friendly than ever, with improved layout, graphics, charts, full-color photographs, and wheelchair accessibility information.

Continuing to refine an upgrade made to the fourth edition, we've provided information for turning a day visit to hike in the park into a multiday getaway, including insider knowledge about campgrounds and lodging in and around Mount Rainier National Park. See page xxix for details.

Whether your stay at Rainier will be a single day or much longer, you'll appreciate trail triage tips that include extensive "Best" lists and suggestions that point you toward specific trails for specific conditions, experiences, hiking companions, or allotted time. Find these on page xvii.

Some of the most important changes since the previous edition involve getting *into* the park itself: As noted in the introduction, Mount Rainier in spring 2024 announced a new summertime reservation system, details of which are described on page xxiii.

Other upgrades are distinctly aimed at accessibility, with new denotations of trails accessible by mobility devices, further enabling adaptive bikers and other adventurous spirits to get into the woods. While there are no fully accessible (ADA-compliant) trails at Mount Rainier National Park, it has some trails that, to some extent, are doable by wheelchair. Before you head out, be sure to check with staff at the nearest ranger station or visitor center to plan for trail slope, grade, width, surface, and condition, along with any barriers like downed trees, footbridges, or stairs making the trail inaccessible for wheelchair users.

While we're talking about wheels: We've also updated the guide to recognize the growing popularity of mountain, electric, and gravel biking. Starting with the fourth edition, we noted that roads closed to vehicular traffic have lengthened, by miles, access to some of the park's classic day-hike trailheads. We left most of those trails in the guide, in anticipation of more and more folks flocking to them as a combined bike/hike experience. This was a good call. Since then, the growth of different types of outdoor cycling has turned this development even more into a silver lining: roads converted to bike-to-hike trails have brought more diverse groups of recreational enthusiasts to the park. Cyclists—mountain, electric and gravel types—can ride these wide, graded hike-bike trails within park boundaries as the prelude (and postscript) to a hike, or just a ride itself alongside a creek or up to a scenic vista. Just remember that wheeled riding on Mount Rainier National Park's hiking-only trails is not permitted.

Beyond that, some other good news. In this space with the fourth edition, we rejoiced over recovery in the park from devastating flooding in 2003 and 2006, with torrents that took away entire trails and even a popular campground. We're happy to report that no such devastating weather impacted access to the park in the years leading up to this fifth edition.

One exception is notable: High water in 2021 claimed the bridge leading to the magical old-growth forest in the Grove of the Patriarchs Trail, cutting off access to the highlight portion of that classic Northwest day hike, which, because of funding schedules, may not be fully restored until 2026 or beyond. We've left the trail description in this guide with the expectation and hope that it will be repaired, and access restored. (In the short term, we've taken this hike out of "Best" listings for now, in case our hopes are not realized.)

Another exception is worth considering: National Forest Service Road 59 has closed due to numerous large washouts. This has cut off primary access to the Lake George, Goat Lake, and Glacier View hikes (Hikes 8, 9, 10). The Forest Service has promised repairs likely beginning in summer 2025. Check with the Cowlitz Valley Ranger District office before you go.

As always, there's no guarantee that rapid change won't occur without warning on Mount Rainier. It is, lest we forget, a slumbering volcano that could decide on several moments' notice to simply eliminate itself from the landscape. It will never be stable. But the sort of flooding, mudslides, wildfires, and other predicaments that caused major trail damage, then rebuilding, around the park in past years has been mostly absent since the previous edition of this guide. The landscape in succeeding years has actually seen some remarkable healing—the sort of slow-creeping regrowth that can only occur in nature with help from the hands of time.

Please note also that Mount Rainier Park has now gone farther out of its way to note that two preferably unrelated activities, flying drones of any kind and partaking in usage of recreational marijuana, are forbidden inside the park.

The meat and potatoes of this or any guide—trails and their current conditions—have been thoroughly rechecked. But with a nod to the climate-related damages noted above, we encourage visitors to check in with the park and various hiking websites for any short-term conditions of concern.

Contact information in the guide has also been verified, with web links and X (Twitter) feeds added where appropriate.

As always, we appreciate your help in keeping the guide current. Feedback to the authors from readers suggests this guide has proven a useful tool to many hikers, whether longtime park users or first-time visitors. For that we are grateful, and please know that your suggestions and updates are always welcome.

BEST HIKES

Many years ago, the late Harvey Manning, an Eastside Seattle–based legend of the hiking guide craft, told this author that most of us following in his footsteps were doing good work, but too many fell into the "cream-skimmer" category. He was correct: Harvey and his compatriots selected entire river drainages, parks, or wilderness areas and hiked every walkable trail therein, faithfully describing the terrain. While many recent guidebook authors have done some of that, they increasingly have turned to offering advice for modern outdoorspersons who are often more pressed for time, thus short on patience for trial and error.

Helping out with some triage is useful for such hikers—and let's face it, more and more of us fit into the cream-skimmer category (as Harvey predicted). In that spirit—and in the original, prescient Harvey Manning spirit that boots on the ground in great numbers are the best way to keep wilderness wild—we offer the following new "Best" lists to help you match this guide's rich selection of hikes with daily conditions, hiking companions, and desired experiences. Note that the hikes in each list are in no particular order of preference—they all should fit the bill for the experience in question.

Best First "Trail We Wanted to Hike Is Still Snowed In!" Alternatives

NO.	HIKE NAME
1.	Kautz Creek/Indian Henry's Hunting Ground, Nisqually Entrance
3.	Trail of the Shadows, Longmire
25.	Silver Falls Loop, Stevens Canyon Entrance
27.	Eastside Trail

Best "I Only Have Half a Day!" Hikes

NO.	HIKE NAME
12.	Nisqually Vista Trail
14.	Panorama Point/Skyline Loop
20.	Pinnacle Saddle
37.	Sunrise Rim Loop
41.	Burroughs Mountain Loop

Best Family-Friendly Hikes

NO.	HIKE NAME
3.	Trail of the Shadows
8.	Lake George
12.	Nisqually Vista Trail
25.	Silver Falls Loop
29.	Sheep Lake

Best Mobility-Device-Friendly Hikes

NO.	HIKE NAME
3.	Trail of the Shadows (from Longmire)
7.	Round Pass/Westside Road
12.	Nisqually Vista Trail (from Jackson Visitor Center)
14.	Panorama Point/Skyline Loop (from Paradise parking area)
44.	Green Lake Trail (from Carbon River Road to lake turnoff)

Best Waterfall Hikes

NO.	HIKE NAME
5.	Carter/Madcap Falls
6.	Comet Falls/Van Trump Park
16.	Paradise to Narada Falls
25.	Silver Falls Loop
51.	Spray Falls/Spray Park

Best Fall-Color/Berry-Picking Hikes

NO.	HIKE NAME
18.	Paradise Glacier
28.	Naches Peak Loop
31.	Crystal Lakes
38.	Sourdough Ridge/Dege Peak
47.	Cataract Valley Camp/Seattle Park

Best Deep-Forest Plunges

NO.	HIKE NAME
2.	Twin Firs Loop
3.	Trail of the Shadows
22.	Stevens Creek
27.	Eastside Trail
45.	Really Big Tree/Ipsut Pass

Best See-Forever Vistas

NO.	HIKE NAME
11.	High Rock Lookout
14.	Panorama Point/Skyline Loop
30.	Noble Knob
38.	Sourdough Ridge/Dege Peak
40.	Frozen Lake/Mount Fremont Lookout

Best Wildflower-Overload Hikes

NO.	HIKE NAME
1.	Indian Henry's Hunting Ground
17.	Upper Paradise Valley
34.	Glacier Basin Trail
36.	Silver Forest/Emmons Vista
51.	Spray Park

Best Lovely Lake Lunch Spots

NO.	HIKE NAME
19.	High Lakes Loop
21.	Bench and Snow Lakes
29.	Sheep Lake
35.	Palisades Lakes
39.	Goat Lake

USING THIS GUIDE

The beginning of each trail description is intended to give you quick information that can help you decide whether the specific day hike is one that interests you. Here's what you'll find:

Trail Number & Name

Trails are numbered in this guide following a geographical order; see the Overview Map on page vi for general location. Trail names usually reflect those names used by the national park, national forest service, and other land managers. In some cases, portions of very long trails or multiple sections of separate trails may have been combined into a single hike and assigned a new name by the author.

Overall Rating

Assigning an overall rating to a hike is a difficult task, given the fact that one hiker's preferred trail is another's dung-heap. Yet every hike in this guide is worth taking (we're still working on the dung-heap trail guide; it might wind up being online only). Here, the difference between a five-star hike and one with four stars might only be the number and variety of wildflowers along the trail, or the height of the tripping tree roots arrayed on the path before you. The trails in this book are already the best you'll find at Mount Rainier. Some might not be as good as others, but they are all better than the ones we've excluded.

Another problem is attempting to be objective in rating the trails. Some of us are pushovers for trails above timberline, where the wildflowers wave in gentle summer breezes, where mountains claw clouds, where cooling snowfields linger through summer. Hikes with these features may be rated higher than you might rate them. If you're a hiker who loves walking along rattling rivers, padding on rain forest trails softened by mosses while trying to find the sky through a canopy of 300-foot-tall evergreens, you might add one star to every lowland hike listed here, and subtract one star from every alpland hike.

Finally, many factors must be considered in assigning an overall rating. Besides all that aesthetic stuff like scenery and wildlife and Really Big Trees, there are objective criteria like trail condition, length and steepness, and obstacles like creek crossings or deadfall. On the other hand, you can forget all that junk and just take our word for it:

★   This hike is worth taking, even with your in-laws.

★★   Expect to discover socially and culturally redeeming values on this hike. Or, at least, very fine scenery.

★★★   You would be willing to get up before sunrise to take this hike, even if you were up late streaming the night before.

★★★★   Here is the Häagen-Dazs of hikes; if you don't like ice cream, a hike with this rating will give more pleasure than any favorite comfort food.

★★★★★   The aesthetic and physical rewards are so great that hikes given this rating are forbidden by most conservative religions.

Distance

The distance listed is round-trip, exclusive of any side trips to other features mentioned along the way. If these excursions off the main trail are longer than about 0.2 mile, that distance will be mentioned in the description of the hike.

Hiking Time

This is an estimate of the time it takes the average hiker to walk the trail, round-trip. Since none of us are average hikers, you may feel free to ignore this entry. For the most part, however, the pace on the trail is calculated at about 2 miles per hour. Times are estimated conservatively; even so, this rate might slow on trails with significant elevation gain. (Some ultralight, overamped trail runners will wonder what sort of trail slug came up with such ridiculously long hiking times—and we're okay with that.)

Elevation Gain

This is a calculation of the total number of feet you'll have to climb on the trail. Don't assume that all of the elevation will be gained on the way to your destination. Some of these trails actually lose elevation on the way and gain it on the return, or alternately gain and lose elevation along the way. The certainty is that on a round-trip hike, you always gain the same amount of elevation that you lose.

High Point

This is the highest point above sea level you'll reach on any given hike. In a few cases, this might be the trailhead.

Difficulty Level

Here's another tough one. Experienced hikers might find a hike rated "Moderately Difficult" to be only "Moderate," while beginning trekkers might rate the same hike "Difficult." As with the hiking times, noted above, the difficulty of individual hikes was rated conservatively.

The terms used here are:

- ♦ **Easy:** Few, if any, hills; generally between 1 and 4 miles, round-trip; suitable for families with small children. In some cases at Rainier, these trails are even paved.

- ♦♦ **Moderate:** Longer, gently graded hills; generally 4 to 6 miles long, round-trip.

- ♦♦♦ **Moderately Difficult:** Steeper grades; elevation changes greater than about 1,000 feet; between 6 and 9 miles long, round-trip.

- ♦♦♦♦ **Difficult:** Sustained, steep climbs of at least 1 mile; elevation gain and loss greater than 1,500 feet; usually more than 9 miles long, round-trip. Your antiperspirant might may fail you.

- ♦♦♦♦♦ **Extreme:** Sustained steep climbs; distances greater than 10 miles, round-trip, or shorter hikes with special conditions requiring extreme care, such as loose rock or snow crossings. These trails will provide a rigorous test of your hiking skills and muscles.

Wheelchair Accessibility

While there are no fully accessible (ADA-compliant) trails at Mount Rainier National Park, it has some trails that are accessible to those using mobility devices, generally measured by a trail's grade, slope, and surface hardness. Individual results may vary, though, because there is no universal way of measuring barrier-free trails. Check with the ranger station or visitor center before you hit the trail.

Yes: Under optimal maintenance conditions, all (or part) of the hike may be accessible by some mobility devices.

No: Indicating a trail is not wheelchair-friendly means it may have barriers to accessibility.

Trail Accessibility

Here you'll find when the trail for any given hike is accessible. Some trails may be open year-round, while others are open seasonally. For hikes listed as open year-round, check trail conditions and snow levels anyway. They might not be fully accessible when snow accumulates at uncommonly low elevations.

Permits/Contact

This entry will tell you whether you need any permits to hike the trail, and whom to contact for more information. As of spring 2024, advance reservations just to enter popular gateways at the park are now required, as part of a park "test." The entrances requiring reservations are: the Paradise corridor via the Nisqually and Stevens Canyon entrances, and the White River and Sunrise entrances.

Reservations are required from the Friday before Memorial Day through Labor Day weekend, and can be made in advance via www.recreation.gov, or by calling (877) 444-6777. For late arrivals, the park will release a block of reservations every day at 7 p.m. for the following morning.

What does a reservation get you? Entrance for one personal vehicle, with a two-hour window to enter the park. There's no required departure time. Each reservation comes with a $2 fee, beyond the normal entrance fee. And you can't pay with cash. Visitors with lodging or camping reservations do not need a timed entry reservation and can enter the park any time after 1 p.m. on the day their stay begins. Likewise, visitors with wilderness, research, or special use permits also do not need a timed entry reservation.

Less-traveled areas of the park, such as Ohanapecosh, Tipsoo Lake, Carbon River, and Mowich Lake, do not require reservations. Check the park website for updates before you go.

With all that established, day hiking in Mount Rainier National Park is still free. Sort of. Most of the trails in this guide are found inside the Nisqually, Stevens Canyon, White River, and Carbon River entrances, where, in addition to that new reservation requirement, a day-use fee (presently $30 per carload, good for seven consecutive days) is collected if not paid in advance. Be advised that, since the fourth edition of this guide, the park has gone cashless; bring your credit or debit card or purchase online in advance.

Frequent park visitors usually fork over $55 for an annual Rainier pass or $80 for an annual Federal Lands Pass granting admission to all US national parks for one year. Other entrance fees include a $15 walk-up or bicycle pass or a $25 pass for motorcycles, good for seven consecutive days.

The park requires permits for overnight backpackers—and charges fees for advance backcountry campsite reservations. (Note: the process has changed in recent years, with the reservation system moving online; see the park's website for the latest information.) But at this writing, no permits or fees are required for day hikers. These regulations are always subject to revision, though: call before you go. Also note that some trails in this guide fall outside national park boundaries and require the purchase of a Northwest Forest Pass, sold by the US Forest Service and private vendors (for $30 per year at the time of this writing). These trails are so noted.

Maps

The two most popular types of maps, United States Geological Survey (USGS) "quads" and Green Trails, are listed for each hike. Maps are available at outdoor retailers, park visitor centers, and from other sources. Many hikers now use GPS devices or internet map servers to download USGS maps or print their own customized maps from software. We advise taking one and not relying on an electronic mapping device. Or if you insist on having one of those, bring a map as well.

Each hike in this book includes a trail map of the route, featuring parking and trailhead, alternate routes, direction, elevation profile, and more. Our maps are based most often on USGS; use the following legend:

℗	Parking Area
——	Road
-------	Trail Route
....	Alternate Route
�	Direction of Travel
↱	Turn Around Point
=	Bridge
5880'	Elevation
	Contour Interval 40 Feet/Scale Varies

Trail Notes

Look here for a quick guide to trail regulations and features: leashed dogs okay; off-leash dogs okay; no dogs; bikes allowed; kid-friendly; good views. Rainier hikers should note up front that pets and mountain bikes are not allowed on any trails within Mount Rainier National Park, but are allowed on a few of this guide's hikes outside park boundaries.

After the at-a-glance overview of each hike, you'll find detailed descriptions of the following:

The Hike

This section is an attempt to convey the feel of the trail in a sentence or two, including the type of trail and whether there's a one-way hiking option.

Getting There

You'll either find out how to get to the trailhead or, God forbid, become hopelessly lost. The elevation at the trailhead is also included here. Most of the trailhead directions will get you to the trailhead from the nearest national park entrance station. Here are some guidelines for getting to those entrances:

In the summer, Mount Rainier is approached by two main access routes: Highways 7 and 706 from the Puyallup/South Tacoma area (to the Nisqually Entrance, Longmire, and Paradise), and Highway 410 from Enumclaw (take Highway 18 to Enumclaw from Interstate 5) beyond Crystal Mountain Boulevard to the White River Entrance and Sunrise. Note that the upper portions of the latter route to Sunrise usually are not open until approximately July 4th. Allow about 2.5 hours from the Seattle area via either route (sorry, traffic snarls not included) when snow isn't a concern.

Snowshoers or cross-country skiers sharp enough to turn some of this guide's hikes into winter routes should note that, in the winter, Highway 410 (Chinook Pass Highway) closes near the national park border, at the Crystal Mountain Boulevard turnoff. That leaves Highway 706 as the only winter park entrance—the Park Service keeps the highway open to Longmire all winter, and endeavors to plow the path to Paradise every day. Chains often are required above Longmire in winter and are required to be carried in all vehicles from November 1 to May 1.

The park has three other summer entrances, whose opening dates vary depending on snowpack. The Stevens Canyon Entrance is on Highway 123 (Cayuse Pass Highway) on the southeast side of the park. This entrance can be reached via US 12 from the south or Highways 410 and 123 from the east, via Enumclaw or Yakima. (Highways 410 and 123 are closed in the winter.) On the northwest side of the park, the Carbon River Road, the upper portion of which is now closed permanently to traffic, and the Mowich Lake Road are unpaved entrances to the scenic (and less heavily visited) north side. Both are accessed via Highway 165, which runs south into the park from Buckley and Wilkeson. These roads are open summer only, and often are in rough condition. The future of both as auto-accessible roads is in doubt.

The Carbon River Road has long been beset by natural calamities. Built below the river grade in places, the old road has washed out repeatedly inside the national park boundary. The final blow came in the deluge of November 2006, which prompted the National Park Service, after much study and deliberation, to cry "Uncle!" and give up on rebuilding the upper Carbon River Road, once and for all. Since 2014, the road has been closed to vehicle traffic at the Carbon River Entrance, with the old Carbon River Road renamed the Carbon River Hike/Bike Trail. For more information, check in at the relocated Carbon River Road, 5.5 miles east of the Mowich Lake Road (SR 165) junction, about 2.5 miles before the park boundary. Hikers should stop here for information and/or permits (for overnighters bound for Ipsut Creek Camp, the former auto campground about 4.9 miles away at the end of the road), then proceed to the park boundary to park and either walk or mountain bike the road-turned-path to local trailheads.

The closure makes sense, given the road's constant problems. But unfortunately, it adds 5 miles each way to formerly short, spectacular day hikes departing from Ipsut Creek Campground, which now has been converted to an attractive backcountry campsite. On the other hand, many people look at this as an opportunity: the closed portion of the road is one of very few scenic places inside the park where one can ride a mountain bike, electric bike, increasingly popular gravel bike, or adaptive mountain bike for wheelchair users. (Note, however, that bikes, human-powered or motorized, remain forbidden on trails that depart from the road.) And what were unique, short hikes to destinations such as the snout of the Carbon Glacier are now even more unique bike/hike options inside Rainier's boundaries. Like it or not, it's the way it is, and not likely to change. The downside: it adds 10 miles round-trip to most day hikes in the area. The upside, for riders: It's 10 miles of open road, and mostly downhill all the way out!

That raised a serious question for this guide: do those hikes still fit the parameters as "day hikes"? The answer is yes—just long ones, for most people probably assisted by a bicycle, which can cover 10 miles for each hike. Surely the road closure will limit the numbers of people who will venture into the Carbon drainage. But the payoff for those who do will be that much more pronounced, partially due to the reduced crowds. Beginning with the third edition of this guide, the round-trip mileages for each trail in the Carbon River region were permanently updated to reflect the additional mileage. They remain in the guide as unique hiker/biker options in this fifth edition.

Likewise, the park's oft washed out West Side Road, which follows the turbulent Tahoma Creek drainage on the southwest side of the mountain, has been permanently closed by the Park Service at a large washout 3.3 miles above its beginning off Highway 706, just inside the Nisqually Entrance. An entire series of spectacular day hikes emanating from the West Side Road have thus become long walks—too long, in most cases, for the average day hiker, even if you employ a mountain bike to get from the washout to the trailhead (where the bike must be left). Much of the road has been repaired—Park Service vehicles seem to have no problems traveling it.

But park managers say frequent outbursts from the South Tahoma Glacier make it too dangerous for private auto travel. An oft-floated proposal to run a hiker's shuttle bus from the road closure to popular trailheads along the route now appears to be a flight of fancy; no federal funding has ever materialized. As a result, we've once again left some of the otherwise grand day hikes emanating from the upper reaches of West Side Road out of this guide, because they exceed the mileage and time guidelines we've established for a day-hiking treatise. But we've included those West Side Road hikes still within a day hiker's reach, and we've even suggested making a fun day hike out of the lower portions of the road itself—see Round Pass (Hike 7).

Note that the park's long-term plans still call for shuttle service to Sunrise, Paradise, the upper Mowich Lake Road, and other popular destinations—and possible auto restrictions in the same places. We'll believe that when we see it! For updates on road conditions, call (360) 569-2211, the park's recorded information line. Or look for updated road-condition Tweets from the Washington State Department of Transportation (@wsdot) and Mount Rainier National Park (@MountRainierNPS).

The Trail

Here's where you'll get the blow-by-blow, mile-by-mile description of the trail. It's information your feet will find useful, and we apologize if, every now and then, we take time to recognize a Really Big Tree or an awesome view, since you'll probably recognize these features without much coaching.

Going Farther

In this section, you can learn about good options to take a longer hike along the same trail. Interesting side trips can be found here, too. And if there's a nearby campground that could get you on the trail sooner, or a great place to stay while exploring area trails, it also will be mentioned. Not every hike includes this section.

CAMPING AND LODGING

Thanks—or no thanks—to the increasingly long commutes to and from Rainier from the Puget Sound lowlands due to what has become chronic traffic congestion, single-day trips to The Mountain and back are becoming less feasible. Time will tell whether a new reservation system just to get in the park will help with that, or hinder. Either way, it's not much of a relaxing escape to awaken at 4 a.m. so you can hit the road early to avoid traffic, spend the day in the park, and then battle traffic coming home, all in one stretch. Accordingly, multiple-day stays in or near the park have become more attractive, even for the dyed-in-the-wool day hiker.

With that in mind, here's a rundown of the best overnight options for national park visitors.

Camping

Call us biased. It might be a reflection of our literally lifelong history of hiking and camping in the park, but despite the need to plan well ahead to snag a campsite for which competition is often fierce, we're firm believers in camping as the go-to option for Rainier visits. This is especially true for those who live in the area and have all the requisite gear. Camping options inside and adjacent to the park are relatively minimalist, compared to some locations. But there are some splendid "front-country" (as opposed to wilderness, hike-in) camps in and around Rainier.

Inside the park, the vast majority of campsites are found at Rainier's two largest campgrounds: Cougar Rock, in the Nisqually drainage between Longmire and Paradise, and Ohanapecosh, on the Ohanapecosh River near the park's Stevens Canyon Entrance off Highway 123 (for travel directions, see Getting There, page 92). Between them, they contain 361 campsites, and if you're guessing you'll need a reservation for summertime visits, you're way ahead of us. Which is the best? That's up to you and your take on their distinct differences.

How Big's Your Rig? It Matters

Before we get into details, an important note about whether your camping trip should include campgrounds inside the park at all: Car-camping sites inside Mount Rainier National Park are sized primarily for tent camping; many also are suitable for camping in a smaller RV or trailer. If you're driving a giant Class A motorhome or diesel pusher, you *might* be able to shoehorn into a site at Cougar Rock or Ohanapecosh. But it also could get very ugly. The spaces, with a few exceptions, simply aren't designed for big rigs and offer no popular services such as RV hookups. Caveat: those who visit the camps often and have scouted out the relative handful of appropriate sites can and do book them in advance and fully enjoy them. But we don't recommend it for first-time visitors or newbies to the process. That said, your author usually brings a Coleman tent trailer, which, when extended, is about 18 feet long and fits comfortably within many appropriate spaces in both campgrounds.

So, where to stay inside the park? Some factors make the choices obvious.

If you plan to spend most of your visit in and around Longmire or Paradise, **Cougar Rock** is a no-brainer. It's wonderfully centrally located between the two popular visitor spots and is across the road from a convenient entrance to one of the park's most popular trail networks. (From here, it's easy to hike downhill to Longmire or up to the splendid Paradise Valley via Narada Falls. See the Carter and Madcap Falls trail listing on page 17.)

Set in a subalpine forest at 3,180 feet, Cougar Rock has a distinctively "alpine" feel—one of its charms. While it suffers from the closely bunched campsites and a lack of amenities typical of national park campgrounds of its era (it has water and flush toilets but no RV hookups or even coin-op showers), it compensates with location, location, location—one that includes a fair number of peekaboo views of Rainier's summit dome.

Cougar Rock's 173 sites are listed as accommodating RVs to 35 feet (see note above on size, however) and most offer little privacy—a big factor for tent campers, especially. But most of you are here to hike, not lounge next to the fire on that new inflatable couch, correct? Correct.

The campground, located 8.3 miles beyond the Nisqually Entrance, about 2.3 miles above Longmire, has piped water, flush toilets, an RV dump station, an amphitheater, and few other amenities. Group sites for 12 or more campers also are available. Stays are limited to 14 days here and at other Mount Rainier National Park campgrounds. At this writing, campsites within the park were $20 per night. Reservations (which can be made up to 6 months in advance by calling (877) 444-6777 or www.recreation.gov) are advised, and will be essential from spring through early fall. The campground typically is open from late May to October.

For those visiting the southeast corner of the park or seeking a splendid base for a longer stay to make day trips around the entire region, **Ohanapecosh** is a popular choice. A bit slower paced than Cougar Rock, Ohanapecosh lies in deep forest at 1,900 feet, straddling both sides of the beautiful Ohanapecosh River—a rare Rainier stream that is not fed by glacial runoff and thus maintains a striking aquamarine color nearly all year. While not popular with sun lizards, this shady riverfront camp is a special place, with stunning day hikes (see Silver Falls Loop, page 92, and temporary shuttered Grove of the Patriarchs, page 88) beginning right from the campground.

The camp's 188 sites are spread across eight heavily forested loops. Like Cougar Rock, privacy is at a minimum here; expect to get acquainted with your neighbors. Some of the best sites, in our mind, are found in Loop C, where a handful sit on a bluff overlooking the river. Sites 18–21 in Loop C offer what feels more like backcountry camping along the banks of the river itself.

If you're camping in an RV, loops E to H, on the river's far side, offer the best choices fit wise.

The campground is located 5 miles north of the Highway 123/ Highway 12 junction near Packwood. During summer months, visitors from the Seattle area also can reach the campground via State Route 706 (Stevens Canyon Road) from the west or SR 410 (Chinook Pass Highway) from the north. Like Cougar Rock, reservations here for summer visits are essential. The camp is open from late May to late October.

The national park's other large camping area, **White River**, is more cramped and more rustic in a classic car camping sort of way. But it's extremely popular among regular visitors to the Sunrise area and day hikers, backpackers, and climbers bound for destinations up the White River, including the Summerland/Panhandle Gap area, the Emmons Glacier, and the ever-popular Glacier Basin, as well as the summit of the mountain itself via Camp Schurman and the Emmons Glacier route.

This camp's 88 sites are decidedly designed for tent campers or extremely tiny RVs and are offered first-come, first-served. With the hyperactive White River flowing nearby and a mountaineering vibe from its status as a jumping-off point for the ice-axe crowd, this can be a fun camping venue; campers seeking to try out that new small-footprint backpacking tent will feel right at home here.

The campground has piped water and flush toilets but no dump station or other amenities. Maximum RV length is listed at 27 feet, with 18 feet for trailers, but we think that's an optimistic estimate. Because of the elevation (4,400 feet), White River camp gets chilly at night even in the summer. And the lack of reservations can make landing a site a crapshoot. (If you get locked out, a good alternative is Silver Springs, outside the park boundary (see page xxxv).

White River, open from late June to late September, is located 5 miles west of the park's White River (Sunrise) Entrance, reached by driving 43 miles east of Enumclaw on State Route 410.

With the 2006 destruction of Sunshine Point, a flood-ravaged campground that was never replaced, the only other remaining auto-accessible camp inside the park is **Mowich Lake**, a remote camp with 13 walk-in sites in the park's northwest corner. The sites are primitive but picturesque, with waterfront lake and summit views. It's a great basecamp for exploring Spray Falls, Spray Park, Seattle Park, and the Carbon Glacier, or a launching point for the famed 93-mile Wonderland Trail around the mountain.

This camp is first-come, first-served, with vault toilets and tables but no fire rings (fires are not allowed). Note that, at 4,929 feet, it usually does not melt out until early July but remains open until early October.

Mowich Lake is at the end of the 17-mile Mowich Lake Road, which is often rough and washboarded. The road begins just beyond the Carbon River Gorge Bridge on State Route 165, in the vicinity of the towns of Buckley and Carbonado (reached via SR 410 from Puyallup).

Last and in some ways least, for car campers, is the **Ipsut Creek Campground**. Ipsut, set in the high drainage of the Carbon River in the northwest corner of the park, is no longer a car-camping site, thanks to the aforementioned permanent closure of the Carbon River Road, 5 miles downstream. But it's a popular overnight spot for those who want to carry their gear by foot or mountain bike (a new use for that kiddie trailer sitting in the garage?) up from the road closure. And it's a great base for exploring the many popular day hikes in this less traveled corner of the park. You'll need a park Wilderness Permit to camp here. They can be obtained online via the national park website or, if available, in person at the Carbon River Ranger Station.

Public Campgrounds Outside the Park

Savvy campers and frequent visitors often leave the national park campsites to the tourists, instead aiming for a favorite site in a series of US Forest Service or other publicly owned camps located outside the park entrance but still near many of Mount Rainier's prime attractions and hiking trails.

On the Nisqually (State Route 7) side, these options include, in order of encounter from west to east on SR 7:

Alder Lake Park/Rocky Point Campground (206 sites; 144 full or partial utility hookups; reservations at (833) 290-8180 or www.mytpu .org), a Tacoma Power–run complex on the Nisqually River near the 330-foot Alder Dam, is a pleasant spot with two camping areas, a boat launch (check water levels), a group camp, and other amenities, including RV hookups. The main campground is at the junction of State Route 7 and School Road, near the Alder Parks Store, just west of the SR 7/ SR 706 junction at Elbe. Rocky Point is 4 miles west on SR 7. (These campgrounds are open year-round except Dec. 20–Jan. 1.) Call (360) 569-2778 for information or (888) 502-8690 for lake levels.

Big Creek, a pleasant Forest Service camp (29 sites; no hookups; RVs to 22 feet; reservations at (877) 444-6777 or www.recreation .gov), offers campsites with better spacing and more privacy than most national park sites and is close enough to the park entrance to put day hikes in the Paradise area within easy reach. Sized primarily for tent campers, it does accommodate RVs to 35 feet in some sites and also offers three double-sized "family" sites, allowing group camping with two vehicles. Big Creek has pit toilets and piped water, sits at 1,818 feet, and is 4 miles south of Ashford (about 23 miles north of Packwood, for US Highway 12 travelers) via State Route 706 and Forest Road 52. It's open from mid-May to late September. Call the Gifford Pinchot National Forest's Cowlitz Valley Ranger District, (360) 497-1100, for more information.

On the northeast (Crystal Mountain) side of the park, accessed by State Route 410, the best car-camping options for those bound for Sunrise-area destinations are a pair of Forest Service campgrounds along the White River:

Dalles (46 sites; no hookups; RVs to 21 feet; reservations at (877) 444-6777 or www.recreation.gov), sits in an old-growth forest, making it shady and cool in the summertime (also dark and gloomy in the offseason). Campsites are found on both sides of SR 410; half can be reserved through the federal website, the other half are first-come, first-served. This campground has pit toilets, piped water, and a short, barrier-free nature trail. Open Memorial Day through Labor Day, Dalles is 26 miles southeast of Enumclaw on SR 410, about 7 miles north of the North Arch (Sunrise) Entrance to the national park. Call the Mount Baker–Snoqualmie National Forest's Snoqualmie Ranger District, (360) 825-6585, for more information.

Nearby **Silver Springs** (56 sites; no hookups; RVs to 30 feet; reservations at (877) 444-6777 or www.recreation.gov) is one of the nicer camping destinations adjacent to Mount Rainier National Park and is conveniently located near Crystal Mountain and Sunrise area day hikes. The campsites here, remodeled and repaved in recent years, are more user-friendly than most found in national park campgrounds and offer decent privacy in a forested area along the White River. A half-dozen sites here are double-sized "family" sites allowing group camping with two vehicles. A group camp also is available. A majority of sites can be reserved in advance. The campground has pit toilets and piped water. Open from late May to mid-September, Silver Springs is 32 miles southeast of Enumclaw on SR 410—about a mile north of the North Arch (Sunrise) Entrance to the national park.

For hikers exploring the Chinook Pass area of Mount Rainier, a series of US Forest Service campgrounds are found along SR 410, on the east side of the Chinook Pass summit. Those within closest commuting distance of the park are **Lodgepole**, **Pleasant Valley**, **Hell's Crossing**, and **Cedar Springs**, all smaller, rustic camps with sites reservable through www.recreation.gov. Call Wenatchee National Forest's Naches Ranger District, (509) 653-1401, for details.

Finally, in the park's southeast corner, best accessed via State Route 123 (seasonal Cayuse Pass), or US Highway 12 (White Pass), a popular alternative to camping at the park's crowded Ohanapecosh Campground is the Forest Service run **La Wis Wis** (122 sites; no hookups; RVs to 24 feet; reservations at (877) 444-6777 or www.recreation.gov).

It's a lovely spot, located near the confluence of the Ohanapecosh and Cowlitz Rivers. Campsite privacy here makes La Wis Wis popular with tent campers, but some pull-through campsites, particularly in the waterfront Hatchery Loop, are comfortable for fairly large RVs. The campground has pit and flush toilets, piped water, a picnic area, a large group camp, and decent river-fishing access. Closed for construction in 2023, it was scheduled to reopen in 2024 with a new water system and water lines, a new toilet, and other upgrades

Short trails lead from the camp to the Blue Hole of the Ohanapecosh River, as well as Purcell Falls. The camp is open from mid-May to late September, and reservations are strongly recommended. La Wis Wis, at 1,243 feet, is on Forest Road 1272, about 6 miles northeast of Packwood via US 12. Call the Gifford Pinchot National Forest's Cowlitz Valley Ranger District, (360) 497-1100, for more information.

Lodging
Camping is not high on the agenda for many, of course, and even ardent campers sometimes prefer clean sheets. Fortunately, just like its campfire-ring destinations, Mount Rainier National Park offers a range of overnight lodging options, both inside it and immediately adjacent to it. Inside the park, visitors have their choice of two classic lodges, both run by contractor Mount Rainier Guest Services and both upgraded to more modern standards than their previous, rather uncomfortably rustic, incarnations.

The **National Park Inn** at Longmire is popular with Paradise-area visitors, and is the only park accommodation open year-round, making it a favored wintertime retreat for hikers who can't resist following some of their favorite trails in the snowy months, wearing skis or snowshoes. The pleasant three-story structure in the little company-town-feeling wayside of Longmire has 25 guest rooms, a full-service dining room, and a general store located in a 1911 log cabin. In summer, the inn's front porch, fitted appropriately with rustic rockers, is a popular spot to watch the alpenglow fade from Rainier.

Having stayed in or visited many of the classic national park lodges of the West, we can attest that the inn lacks the authentic feel of some of those destinations. But it's a pleasant spot with small but comfortable rooms and touches such as a large stone fireplace and a communal library/game room that make it feel more like a lodge than a hotel. That point is further driven home by the lack of televisions, phones, or internet access anywhere within the premises (sorry, kids!).

With the exception of two accessible suites, all guest rooms are on the second floor and accessed by stairs. The rooms, all non-smoking, come with or without bathrooms, and at this writing ranged from $210 to $432 per night. (Note: This price has nearly doubled since the fourth edition in 2019.)

The National Park Inn's location, near park administrative offices and other structures in the Longmire Historic District, is ideal; day hiking trails such as the popular Trail of the Shadows begin literally off the front porch. And Paradise is a short drive away. The village is named after James Longmire, a pioneer settler who used Native American trails to access the area, staked a claim here, built a cabin, and began plans for a lodging facility near a nearby hot springs in 1883. The current inn once served as an annex to the larger original National Park Inn, destroyed by fire in 1926. It was renovated in 1936 and 1990.

Far grander in size, scope, and location, the historic 1916 **Paradise Inn**, located smack dab amidst the splendor of the alpine meadows at Paradise, traded on its reputation as one of the "Great Lodges of the West" since it opened in 1917. While its undersized guest rooms with thin walls and stale furnishing lived up to the "rustic" side of that theme, the well-worn inn lagged behind in the "great" department for many decades, prompting many visitors to sigh and advise: "Come for the park, not the hotel." Renovations in 2006 and 2007 and a two-year, $24.5 million restoration completed in 2019 helped narrow that gap.

The hewn-log (Alaska cedars, fire-killed in the Narada Falls area) construction and scale of this inn truly do give it the classic Western lodge look and feel, and the renovations brought guest accommodations up a notch in quality. Set against a slope festooned with the otherworldly colors of alpine wildflowers in summer months and blaze-orange underbrush in the fall, it would never be built at its current locale today. But that is to the decided advantage of the inn's guests, who can walk a few paces from the grand lobby to find day hiking trails on par with any for natural beauty.

Adjacent to the main Paradise parking area at 5,400 feet, the summers-only Paradise Inn still gets its fair share of the mountain's notoriously fickle weather; nobody with prior experience comes here at any time of the year without the requisite clothing layers appropriate to an alpine environment. But when the sun is out and the mountain is on full display, few alpine lodgings inspire the sort of wonder found here. Open from mid-May through September, the facility offers 42 rooms in the main lodge and an additional 79 in the lodge annex built in 1920. Rooms at this writing were $210 to $459 per night. Like its sister lodging in Longmire, Paradise Inn has no televisions, telephone service, or broadband, but it does have a full-service restaurant, bar, and other amenities. Check out the 14-foot grandfather clock in the lobby. You can't miss it.

Reservations for both historic inns can be made at www.mtrainier guestservices.com or by calling (855) 755-2275.

Lodging Outside the Park

Given the tourist-scale prices and amenities inside the park, most locals opting to go the cushy route on multiday hiking trips to Mount Rainier will opt for lodging outside the park proper. Options, especially on the stretch of State Route 706 between Elbe and Ashford, just outside the Nisqually Entrance on the Paradise side of the park, are many. More than 30 mostly small-scale accommodations are found here, ranging from small, rustic log cabins to expansive lodge and condominium suites, bed-and-breakfast facilities, and even a climber's bunkhouse operated by the Whittaker family of mountain-climbing fame (in Ashford proper).

Another cluster of about a dozen varied lodging options is found in the Crystal Mountain ski area on the northeast (Sunrise) side of the park, accessed by State Route 410. Conveniently, all these park-perimeter accommodations can be explored and booked through visitrainier.com (@visitmtrainier on X, formerly Twitter). For information about lodging and dining at the ski resort (which also offers summer mountain biking, a Rainier gondola ride, and other activities), see CrystalMountainResort.com or AltaCrystalResort.com.

BE CAREFUL

It is all too easy on a warm, sunny day on the trail to forget all of the stuff you ought to be carrying in your pack. Day hikers, especially, are likely to leave that extra layer or Gore-Tex parka in the trunk. Some folks even forget that most essential item—a hiking partner. Never hike alone.

Virtually every time, day hikers who forget one or two of the basic rules for safe wilderness travel return to the trailhead smiling and healthy. No trail cop is going to cite you for negligent hiking if you have only nine of the so-called "Ten Essentials," or if you hit the trail without registering or telling someone where you're going.

Perhaps the only weighty argument anyone can make to convince another day hiker to follow the rules for safe travel in the outdoors is this: remember the annual, avoidable tragedies that occur because hikers ignore those rules and become news headlines instead.

The Ten Essentials

First—no matter the distance or difficulty of the hike—please carry in your pack the Ten Essentials, developed years ago by the Seattle-based mountaineering group The Mountaineers. Don't leave home without these:

- A topographic **map** of the area.
- A **compass**, and the ability to use it in conjunction with the map. While they're excellent aids to navigation, portable GPS units are no substitute for a compass that does not require batteries or satellite reception. But if you're handy with one, they surely make a fine "11th Essential" to keep you on course, or keep track of where you have been.

- **Extra clothing**, which should consist of a top and bottom insulating layer and a waterproof and windproof top layer. A hat or cap is absolutely essential; mountaineers will tell you that when your feet are cold, put on your hat. It works.
- To avoid grazing on your **extra food**, try to pick something you would eat only if you were starving, like freeze-dried turnips or breakfast bars that taste like pressed sawdust. Keep a box of energy bars always handy in the cupboard or car.
- Carry a **flashlight** with extra batteries and bulbs or a headlamp, which allows you to swat at the moths that fly into the light without dropping the bloody flashlight. Many of these lights have spare bulbs built-in. Lithium batteries, though more expensive, make excellent spares because their shelf-life is longer than yours, and they last much longer in colder weather.
- You can buy excellent **first-aid kits** that are already assembled. The type of injury, however, that is likely to incapacitate a day hiker may be different from one suffered by a backpacker. If your first aid kit doesn't include wraps for sprains, add an ankle support, and be sure you have some kind of blister treatment.
- **Matches** in a waterproof case are recommended over butane lighters, as both altitude and temperature can affect a lighter's performance.
- Candles work well as a **fire starter**, along with a variety of lightweight commercial products.
- A **pocket knife** is an indispensable tool.
- **Sunglasses** and sunscreen are useful, especially at high altitudes.

In addition to these items, most day hikers never hit the trail without toting some toilet paper in a plastic bag and perhaps some type of bug repellent on summer hikes. A loud emergency whistle is a lightweight addition. A small, insulating "space blanket" makes a nice lunch tablecloth—and could save your life if you have to spend the night. Binoculars are worth their weight simply for watching wildlife, and might help find your route if you become lost. Consider, too, a walking stick of some variety; it can take the stress off your knees on steep downhills, help steady you while crossing streams, and serve a wide variety of other useful purposes, such as a support post for a portable lean-to should you need emergency shelter.

Water

Dehydration is one of the most common ailments that day hikers face. No one should head out on the trail without at least one liter of clean water per person.

You'll find plenty of opportunities to refill your water bottle on most of the hikes outlined in this book. In cases where creek crossings are scarce or obtaining water might be a problem, it will be mentioned in the trail description.

Treat all water in the wilderness as if it were contaminated. The most worrisome problem might be a little critter called *Giardia lamblia*, which can give you a case of the trots that you'll never forget. The most noticeable symptom of giardiasis is "explosive diarrhea." Need you know more? Probably not.

Thankfully, there is an easy way to assure that the water you take from mountain streams and lakes is safe to drink. When used properly, filter pumps eliminate at least 99.9 percent of giardia and other dangerous organisms from the water. A far more convenient addition to filter pumps, especially for day hikers, are the relatively inexpensive water bottles equipped with their own filters. You simply fill the bottle from the stream (taking extreme care not to contaminate the mouthpiece or drinking cap), drop the filter into place and screw on the top, and you're ready to drink filtered water. Conversely, many veteran hikers still choose to forego all this gadgetry and use the old-fashioned method: iodine-tablet water treatments, which come in tablets or crystals. The taste might be objectionable to some, but it's a guaranteed way to kill giardia and other water-borne bugs—something a filter, especially an improperly used or maintained one, is not.

Weather

In any mountains, weather can change rapidly and with little warning. On most any alpine hike in the fall, you can get snowed upon, rained upon, sleeted upon, blown around, and finally sunburned—all in the span of a day. Hikers in Washington's mountains have frozen to death in July and drowned in the afternoon while fording flood-filled rivers that were shallow in the morning. Mother Nature is most often a friendly, generous old lady who bakes cookies and bread for you, but when you least expect it she puts on a goalie's mask and whacks at you with an icicle or lightning bolt. Rain, wind, and exposure can combine forces to produce hypothermia in no time in Washington's Cascades, particularly in alpine areas, where it's always a good idea to carry waterproof, windproof clothing—no matter how nice the weather looks when you depart. Wind chill and hypothermia kill far more people in Washington's Cascades than any other hazard.

In the specific case of Rainier, add to this menace unexpected snowstorms and other natural not-niceties. It's been said so often that it approaches cliché, but it's true: the mountain is such a giant physical presence, it literally creates its own weather. "Winter" as most people would normally define it lasts eight or nine months at Rainier. Many trails can be hiked only in a short summer season that lasts from July through October. Even then, bad weather can strike, especially on alpine trails exposed to the elements, which is the case with many of Rainier's most popular hikes.

Other unique challenges offered up by Rainier are avalanches (generally in the spring) and geologic hazards. The latter can range from volcanic events (extremely rare) to flash flooding and mudslides resulting from rapidly melting glaciers (also rare, but always a danger). All of that glacial ice up above makes Rainier an unstable mass of rock and water, some of which is bound to come down rapidly and unpredictably. (An example was at Van Trump Creek, where a huge muddy-debris flow—the result of a long, hot spell melting a glacier—menaced hikers on the popular Comet Falls trail in the late summer of 2001.) Hiking through volcanic creek drainages, especially during protracted hot spells, on glacier-fed rivers or streams, calls for extra caution: If you hear what sounds like a dozen freight trains booming down a canyon toward you, don't do what may come naturally by turning and running downstream. Head for high ground and wait it out. It's also worth remembering that, on warm days, the tiny, trickling stream you hopped over in the morning might become a raging gusher by the time you return in the afternoon.

Rangers interviewed in preparing the fifth edition of this guide noted several deaths in recent years by hikers crossing streams: the Mowich River (South Mowich Crossing), Winthrop Creek on the Wonderland Trail, and the west fork of the White River on the Northern Route trail. Please use caution, and heed the advice of experts: Any negotiable glacial river crossing in the park can be there one day and not the next.

The bottom line: On Mount Rainier, even more so than in other Cascade and Olympic mountain destinations, good planning and preparation are vital. Consult with rangers about weather and trail conditions before you leave. Tell someone where you're going. Don't take on a hike you're not mentally or physically equipped to handle. In other words, use common sense.

Flora & Fauna

For the most part, the animals and plants of Mount Rainier are benign. The most common danger might be an encounter with poison oak, stinging nettles, or, in rare instances, a black bear or a cougar.

Day hikers needn't fear black bears, but should realize these are wild animals that can cause serious injury if provoked. While it's highly unlikely you'll ever have a grizzly bear to worry about, research indicates that a black bear attack, though extremely rare, may more often lead to a fatality. A greater potential danger might be from cougars. Encounters between humans and cougars are believed to be increasing throughout Washington State, but you probably will never see one on the trail.

If you do encounter a bear or cougar, heed the following advice from the Department of Fish and Wildlife:

Bear: Give the bear plenty of room to get away. Never get between a cub and its mother. Avoid eye contact but speak softly to the bear while backing away from it. Try not to show fear and don't turn your back on a bear. If you can't get away from it, clap your hands or yell in an effort to scare it away. If the bear becomes aggressive, fight back using anything at your disposal. Should the attack continue, curl up in a ball or lay down on your stomach and play dead.

Cougar: Don't take your eyes off the cougar. Make yourself appear big by raising your arms above your head, open your jacket if you're wearing one, and wave a stick above your head. If the cougar approaches, yell and throw rocks, sticks, anything you can get your hands on. In the event of an attack, fight back aggressively.

Less dangerous, but more common hazards to day hikers include stinging and biting pests like yellow jackets, particularly in late summer and early autumn, and black flies, mosquitoes, and deer flies. Liberal doses of insect repellent (those with at least some percentage of the chemical "DEET" are most effective) can take care of the mosquitoes and deer flies, but probably won't keep those pesky yellow jackets away.

Poison oak and ivy grow in some areas of the Cascades, mostly in sunny, dry areas. A more common plant pest is stinging nettle, which grows in profusion along many trails but is easily avoided if you recognize it in time.

None of this, of course, should be construed as discouragement. We've been hiking in Rainier for a lifetime, and have yet to get lost in a snowstorm, be menaced by wild animals, attacked by killer bees, or swept away in a glacial runoff. So tighten your bootlaces, shoulder that pack, and get out on one of the hikes that follow.

Etiquette/Ethics

To protect this wonderful landscape so that users in future generations can enjoy it just as much as you, please follow a few simple rules. Stay on established trails, don't cut switchbacks, and stay off sensitive areas. Leave no trace, pack out your trash, and respect other trail users. And because you're having such a great time using Washington's trails, why not volunteer your services by lending a hand on a trail building or repair project?

Happy trails! ■

LONGMIRE/ COUGAR ROCK

---

1. Kautz Creek/Indian Henry's Hunting Ground

RATING	DISTANCE	HIKING TIME
★★★☆☆	**2.0 miles round-trip to Kautz Creek/11.5 miles round-trip to Indian Henry's Hunting Ground**	**1.0 hour/ 6.0 hours**

ELEVATION GAIN	HIGH POINT	DIFFICULTY	♿
250 feet (Kautz) **3,200 feet** (Indian)	**2,469 feet** (Kautz) **5,600 feet** (Indian)	◆◇◇◇◇ ◆◆◆◇◇	**No**

TRAIL ACCESSIBLE
Jan Feb Mar Apr May **Jun Jul Aug Sep Oct Nov** Dec

The Hike

This is a short, pleasant day hike through a forest recovering from a glacial flow on Kautz Creek, or a full day's major ascent to one of Rainier's most memorable wildflower meadow parklands.

Getting There

From the park's Nisqually Entrance on Highway 706, drive about 3 miles toward Longmire on the Longmire-Paradise Road to the large, well-marked Kautz Creek Picnic Area on the right (south) side of the road, elevation 2,400 feet. The path begins across the road from the parking lot.

PERMITS/CONTACT

Entrance fee; no day-hiking passes required/
Longmire Wilderness Information Center, (360) 569-6650

MAPS

Green Trails No. 269, Mount Rainier West; USGS Wahpenayo Peak and Mount Rainier West

TRAIL NOTES

No dogs; first mile very kid-friendly; no bikes

The Trail

This is two hikes in one: The first mile of the trail is an uncommonly easy stroll through a forest area recovering from a massive, muddy outburst from the Kautz Glacier, which destroyed much of the old forest here in 1947. The stream changed paths completely again during violent flooding in 2006; see the interpretive sign along the river near the trailhead. But most of the trail survived intact. The path climbs a gentle mile to a footlog crossing Kautz Creek in an area where the stream's broad, gravelly channel affords plenty of room to stretch out and down that sandwich you packed along. Bring your camera: The Mountain (assuming clear weather, which you probably shouldn't) will be beaming at you from the north. (Winter walkers

The lower portions of the Kautz Creek Trail are a great family walk; the upper parts, a challenging ascent

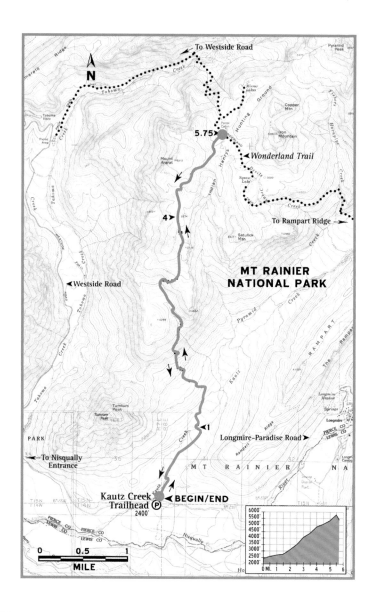

To Westside Road

N

5.75

◄*Wonderland Trail*

To Rampart Ridge ►

4►

MT RAINIER NATIONAL PARK

◄Westside Road

◄1

Longmire–Paradise Road ►

◄To Nisqually Entrance

Kautz Creek Trailhead ◄**BEGIN/END**
2400'

0   0.5   1
MILE

should note that this portion of the trail also has become a popular winter snowshoe route.)

If you're up for much more adventure, though, keep on going. Assuming the footlog has not been washed out by the creek—which can be as cranky as your spouse on tax day—cross the water and get ready to climb. From here, the trail gets narrower, slicker, and, from about the 2.0-mile mark on, much, much, much steeper, switching back through a dark, lush, gorgeous old-growth forest. The grade doesn't let up until about 4.0 miles, when Rainier and surrounding peaks such as 6,010-foot Mount Ararat (on the left) and 5,577-foot Satulick Mountain (on the right) come into view.

After topping out in Indian Henry's splendid alpine meadows at 5,600 feet and **5.0** miles, you'll actually drop about 600 vertical feet over the final 0.75 mile to a junction with the Wonderland Trail and a nearby backcountry patrol cabin.

Going Farther

If your legs are still up for it after the climb, turn left at the Wonderland Trail junction and proceed about a quarter mile through the large meadow to the Mirror Lakes Trail, which leads an additional three-fourths mile and about 100 vertical feet up to a tiny set of lakes below the twin peaks of Iron and Copper Mountains. The picturesque Mirror Lake reflection of Rainier and 6,937-foot Pyramid Peak to the northeast was documented in a famous Asahel Curtis photograph reproduced on a 1934 US postage stamp—ask your granddad if he remembers.

For strong hikers, another option from the Kautz Creek/Wonderland Trail junction is to continue west on the Wonderland and Tahoma Creek Trails for a one-way shuttle hike of 11 miles from the Kautz Creek Picnic Area to the West Side Road. Note that the Tahoma Creek Trail—in days of yore, by far the easiest access to Indian Henry's—is no longer maintained by the park, and can be difficult to negotiate under good conditions and downright dangerous under bad (high water) ones. And it's about a mile-long walk from the Tahoma Creek trailhead to your pickup point, the washout closure 3.3 miles up the West Side Road.

Also, hikers turning east on the Wonderland Trail from back at the Kautz Creek junction can complete a one-way through hike to Longmire via Rampart Ridge (Hike 4) for a total of 12 miles. ■

2. Twin Firs Loop

RATING	DISTANCE	HIKING TIME
★ ★ ★ ☆ ☆	0.5-mile loop	20 minutes

ELEVATION GAIN	HIGH POINT	DIFFICULTY	♿
Minimal	2,500 feet	♦ ◇ ◇ ◇ ◇	No

TRAIL ACCESSIBLE—UNLESS SNOW LEVEL IS BELOW 2,500 FEET
Jan Feb Mar Apr May Jun Jul Aug Sep Oct **Nov Dec**

The Hike
Enjoy a short, easy, little-known trail offering a grand introduction to the giant old-growth Douglas fir and western red cedars found throughout Mount Rainier National Park. This is one of the first leg-stretcher hikes you'll encounter entering the park from the Nisqually Entrance.

Getting There
From the park's Nisqually Entrance on Highway 706, drive about 4 miles (0.9 mile beyond the Kautz Creek trailhead) to a pullout and

PERMITS/CONTACT
Entrance fee; no day-hiking passes required/
Longmire Wilderness Information Center, (360) 569-6650

MAPS
Green Trails No. 301, Randle; USGS Mount Rainier West; but note that these and most other topographic maps do not show this trail

TRAIL NOTES
No dogs; kid-friendly; no bikes

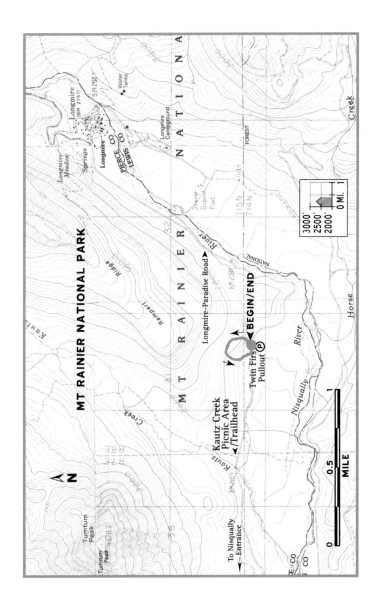

visible interpretive sign on the left (north) side of the road. From Longmire, look for the trailhead about 2 miles west on the right side of the road. The trailhead, elevation 2,465 feet, is not marked by a sign, but interpretive displays mark the spot.

The Trail

Gung-ho mileage burners, keep right on going. Tree huggers? Step right up. The Twin Firs Loop is, quite simply, one of the more peaceful, beautiful—and unknown—nature trails on the south side of Mount Rainier National Park. (We've been visiting the park for decades, but didn't discover this trail until we got around to compiling this guide.) Kids and the creaky kneed will love this walk. If they don't, make them do it over and over again—with you acting as old-growth-forest interpreter—until they do.

From the easy-to-miss trailhead, pull off the road and stretch your road-weary legs in the best way possible: beneath some truly stunning, behemoth Douglas firs and western red cedars. These are some of the largest you're likely to see near a road in the park, with the exception of the much more crowded Grove of the Patriarchs Trail near Ohanapecosh (Hike 24)—temporary closed as of 2021. From its outset, this delightful trail bounces along, slightly uphill, between massive old-growth trees—a perfect example of the "terminal forest" that rings The Mountain.

Unlike most trails in the park, this one is snow-free for much of the year. It's a great fresh-air outing for lodgers at the National Park Inn at Longmire, and can be combined with the first mile of the Kautz Creek Trail (Hike 1) and/or the Trail of the Shadows (Hike 3) walk at Longmire for a fine morning or afternoon of stress-free forest strolling. ■

Old-growth forest provides a welcome respite in any weather

3. Trail of the Shadows

RATING	DISTANCE	HIKING TIME	
★★★☆☆	0.75-mile loop	30 minutes	
ELEVATION GAIN	HIGH POINT	DIFFICULTY	♿
55 feet	2,805 feet	♦◆◆◆◆	Yes

TRAIL ACCESSIBLE—UNLESS SNOW LEVEL IS BELOW 2,750 FEET
Jan Feb Mar Apr May Jun Jul Aug Sep Oct Nov Dec

The Hike
Follow this easy nature trail through a meadow at Longmire that has an interesting history involving the area's first white settlers.

Getting There
From the park's Nisqually Entrance on Highway 706, proceed 6 miles to Longmire and park in the lot behind the National Park Inn, elevation 2,750 feet. The trail begins directly across the Longmire-Paradise Road from the National Park Inn.

The Trail
One of the most popular interpretive trails in the park, the Trail of the Shadows is, as its name implies, a pleasant, shady walk around Longmire Meadow, part of an original homestead claim by the James Longmire family. Longmire, in many ways, was most responsible for the tourist boom at Rainier. On his way to the summit in 1883, he happened upon this meadow and its bubbling mineral springs, which

PERMITS/CONTACT
Entrance fee; no day-hiking passes required/
Longmire Wilderness Information Center, (360) 569-6650

MAPS
Green Trails No. 269, Mount Rainier West; USGS Mount Rainier West

TRAIL NOTES
No dogs or bikes; very kid-friendly; first 0.25 mile is barrier-free

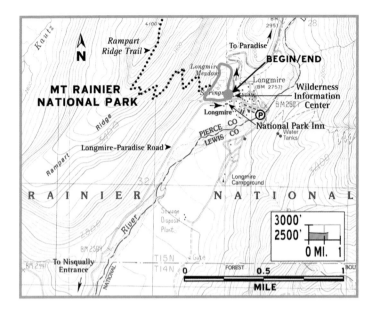

he was marketing to visitors a year later as a source of healing powers (the water reportedly was much warmer then).

The Shadows loop, designed to be walked counterclockwise, is dotted with signs that tell the story of Longmire's establishment here, which eventually included a hotel and other amenities (a printed trail guide is available at the trailhead). The path passes by two mineral springs and an 1888 homestead cabin built by Longmire's son.

This is a pleasant walk all year. In summer, the short spur trail leading to the center of the meadow makes a sublime Mount Rainier photo spot. In October, low vegetation bursts forth with color in Longmire Meadows. Even in the winter, this loop gets plenty of use: It's a good standby, low-elevation walk for those days when the upper mountain is socked in; when snow levels plummet, it makes a grand winter snowshoe or cross-country ski route; or just a stroll through the snowy meadows while you're waiting for snowplows to clear the road to Paradise early on those frosty winter weekend mornings.

Going Farther
The Rampart Ridge Trail (Hike 4) connects on the west side of this loop. ∎

Longmire Meadows offers a spectacular view of Rainier

4. Rampart Ridge Loop

RATING	DISTANCE	HIKING TIME
★★ ☆ ☆ ☆	4.8-mile loop	2.5 hours

ELEVATION GAIN	HIGH POINT	DIFFICULTY	&#9855;
1,300 feet	4,080 feet	♦ ♦ ◇ ◇ ◇	No

TRAIL ACCESSIBLE
Jan Feb Mar Apr May **Jun Jul Aug Sep Oct** Nov Dec

The Hike

This occasionally steep, mostly forested, low-elevation loop on a prominent ridge above the Longmire area serves as a good early-season or foul-weather alternative to alpine hikes.

Getting There

From the park's Nisqually Entrance on Highway 706, proceed 6 miles to Longmire and park in the lot behind the National Park Inn, elevation 2,750 feet. The trail begins on the Trail of the Shadows (Hike 3), directly across the main road from the National Park Inn. Walk that loop clockwise (to the left) one-fourth mile to the well-signed Rampart Ridge trailhead.

The Trail

Although far from the most scenic trail in the park, the Rampart Ridge Loop nonetheless gets a heavy boot-pounding every year for one good reason: its practicality. With a high point of less than 4,100 feet,

PERMITS/CONTACT
Entrance fee; no day-hiking passes required/
Longmire Wilderness Information Center, (360) 569-6650

MAPS
Green Trails No. 269, Mount Rainier West; USGS Mount Rainier West

TRAIL NOTES
No dogs; kid-friendly—but they might get bored; no bikes

The Rampart Ridge trail connects to the Trail of the Shadows nature path

and a route that follows a mostly south-facing slope, this trail usually melts out in June, well before many other popular south-side Rainier destinations, most of which climb to 5,500 feet or above. The loop begins and ends at the Longmire complex, and you can walk it either direction. Going clockwise, however, gives you more face-first views of The Mountain, when it's visible.

Walk the Trail of the Shadows Loop (Hike 3) clockwise, or left, from its trailhead for about a quarter mile to the Rampart Ridge junction. Head up the hill through deep forest on steep switchbacks for about 1.5 miles, when the grade lessens slightly. At about **1.75** miles, watch for a view looking west toward 4,678-foot Tumtum Peak, looming over the far side of the Kautz Creek drainage. A short distance farther,

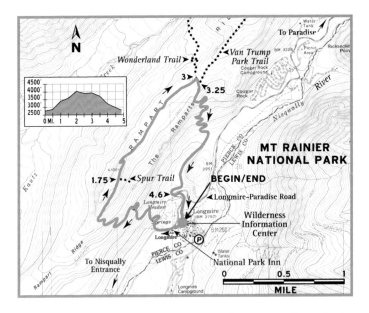

follow the short spur trail to a viewpoint of Rainier, Eagle Peak, the Longmire area and a vast section of the upper Nisqually drainage.

You can turn around here and be happy with a round-trip view hike of 3.6 miles. But you've done most of the hard stuff already, so press on. The path from here flattens out and follows the ridge top northeast, right toward Rainier's summit, for more than a mile, with occasional views into the Kautz drainage on the left. At mile **3.0,** turn right at the Wonderland Trail junction, and in another quarter mile stay right again at the Van Trump Park Trail junction to continue on the Wonderland Trail. It's downhill all the way home from here, a shy 2 miles through pleasant forest, across the road, and then back to Longmire. Note: Carry plenty of water. None is available on the upper part of the route.

Vine maples soak up available light in a forest of firs and cedars

Going Farther

Feeling your oats? Add 9.2 miles and more than 2,100 vertical feet to the hike by turning left (north) at the Wonderland Trail junction, dropping down to a crossing of Kautz Creek, and hoofing it all the way up to Indian Henry's Hunting Ground (Hike 1) to create a 14-mile round-trip. Note that if your plan is to enter Indian Henry's from this side of Rampart Ridge, the practical route is to start on the Wonderland Trail at Longmire and follow it all the way to Indian Henry's, for a strenuous, round-trip hike of 12.4 miles and a total elevation gain of about 2,600 feet. ■

5. Carter/Madcap Falls

RATING	DISTANCE	HIKING TIME	
★★★☆☆	3.0 miles round-trip	1.5 hours	
ELEVATION GAIN	HIGH POINT	DIFFICULTY	♿
535 feet	3,700 feet	◆◇◇◇◇	No
	TRAIL ACCESSIBLE		
	Jan Feb Mar Apr May Jun Jul Aug Sep Oct Nov Dec		

The Hike

This trip is a great choice for Rainier visitors willing to trade views of The Mountain for a pleasant, uncrowded river hike with two fine waterfalls on the Paradise River. This is a good foul-weather alternative to Paradise alpine hikes. It's also the best day hike from Cougar Rock Campground, the park's most popular overnight spot.

Getting There

From the park's Nisqually Entrance on Highway 706, proceed 6 miles to Longmire and another 2.25 miles to the wide shoulder on the right-hand side of the road near Cougar Rock Campground and Picnic Area, elevation 3,165 feet. If parking is not available along the road, continue a short distance to the Picnic Area parking lot on the right. The path begins on a footlog over the Nisqually River.

PERMITS/CONTACT
Entrance fee; no day-hiking passes required/
Longmire Wilderness Information Center, (360) 569-6650

MAPS
Green Trails No. 269, Mount Rainier West; USGS Mount Rainier West

TRAIL NOTES
No dogs; kid-friendly; no bikes

The Trail

Your new Kelty tent is pitched at Cougar Rock Campground, rain fly tauter than a drum. So now what? Lace up your boots, cross the Longmire-Paradise Road outside the campground entrance, and head upstream. This trail—actually a central section of the Paradise River/Wonderland Trail that connects Longmire and Paradise—is a perfect leg stretcher for park newcomers, or a foul-weather backup for frequent visitors who'd been hoping for clear skies up at Paradise. The cloudy-day advantage is obvious: It's tough to get lost on

Madcap Falls is a great destination from Cougar Rock Campground

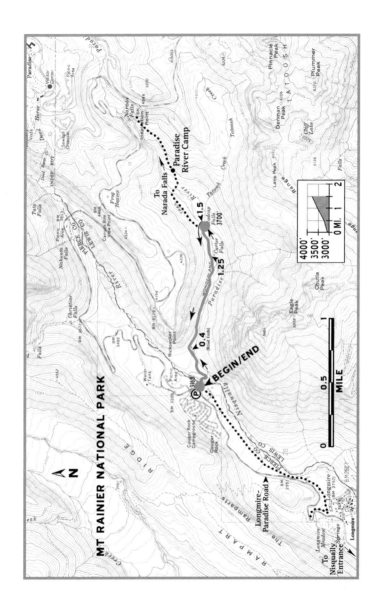

MT RAINIER NATIONAL PARK

N

To
Nisqually
Entrance

Longmire
Springs

Longmire–
Paradise Road

BEGIN/END

P 3165

0.4
(Road Ends)

1.25

Carter
Falls

Madcap
Falls
3700

1.5

To
Narada Falls

Paradise
River Camp

Narada
Falls

0   0.5   1   MILE

0 MI.   1   2

4000'
3500'
3000'

The trail offers a glimpse of severe flooding along the Nisqually River

this route, where the Wonderland Trail crosses the chocolate-milk Nisqually on a series of footlogs before following an old service road at a gentle pace, first parallel to and then away from the raucous river.

The old road ends at about **0.4** mile, where the usually crystal-clear Paradise River announces itself noisily on the right on its way to the Nisqually. From here the path becomes a more standard trail, often following an old wooden water pipe that once fed an electrical generator below. The pace steepens slightly as a sprawling slope of crumbled rock from 5,958-foot Eagle Peak comes into view on the right (low brush puts on a stunning display of color here in the fall). At **1.2** miles, Carter Falls is seen down through the trees on the right at 3,700 feet.

Don't stop here, though. A quarter mile beyond, near the confluence of Tatoosh Creek, is less-obstructed Madcap Falls, a curious gusher in that it really slides down a broad granite step rather than tumbling like a typical falls. The gentle whitewater curtain it creates can make you dizzier than the Zip-A-Whirl at the Puyallup Fair. Turn around here and return the way you came. Or, if you've got a lunch in the pack and/or time on your hands, walk a short distance beyond to an absolutely delightful flat spot in the river just above Madcap Falls. Find broad, smooth rocks that beg to be napped upon and several calm, deep pools that call out to summer bathers.

Going Farther

For a longer hike, continue another 0.6 mile to Paradise River Camp, or 0.9 mile beyond that to Narada Falls, a popular roadside attraction below the Paradise area. Or, turn this trail into a 3-mile, one-way shuttle hike by starting at Narada Falls and going to Cougar Rock. Continue to Longmire for a 4.5-mile one-way hike or, alternately, begin at Longmire and walk 1.7 miles up the Wonderland Trail to the Cougar Rock trailhead. See Hike 16 for more shuttle-hiking options in this area. ■

6. Comet Falls/Van Trump Park

RATING	DISTANCE	HIKING TIME	
★★★★	3.8 miles round-trip to Comet Falls/ 6.0 miles round-trip to Van Trump Park	2.0 hours/ 3.5–4.0 hours	
ELEVATION GAIN 1,600 feet/ 2,200 feet	HIGH POINT 5,200 feet/ 5,800 feet	DIFFICULTY ♦ ♦ ♦ ♦ ♦ ♦ ♦	♿ No

TRAIL ACCESSIBLE

Jan Feb Mar Apr May Jun **Jul Aug Sep Oct** Nov Dec

The Hike

Make a short, steep climb to one of the park's most popular hiking destinations—320-foot Comet Falls—with the option of going on to splendid Van Trump Park or even farther to Mildred Point, an alpine viewpoint.

Getting There

From the park's Nisqually Entrance on Highway 706, drive 6 miles to Longmire and another 4.5 miles to the Van Trump Park trailhead, at 3,600 feet, just below Christine Falls. The lot holds about twenty cars, and is often full on summer days; alternate parking is not available.

The Trail

This route has always been one of the park's most popular trails. But in the summer of 2001 it also became a showcase for just how

PERMITS/CONTACT
Entrance fee; no day-hiking passes required/
Longmire Wilderness Information Center, (360) 569-6650

MAPS
Green Trails No. 269, Mount Rainier West; USGS Mount Rainier West

TRAIL NOTES
No dogs; too steep and rocky for younger kids; no bikes

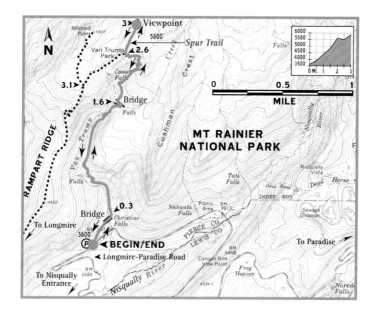

volatile the slumbering giant volcano can be when she stirs in her sleep. The Van Trump Park Trail begins on the highway near Christine Falls and follows Van Trump Creek upward toward its source. That pleasant little creek turned into a deluge in the warm, dry summer of 2001, when a finger of the Kautz Glacier melted rapidly, creating a mud-and-debris flow that cascaded down Van Trump Creek all the way to the Nisqually River.

Hikers at the falls that day were stunned when the water, normally a graceful, white, comet-like plume, turned into an angry, gray, chunky blast, spewing gritty mud for hundreds of yards. Nobody was hurt, thankfully. The trail was closed only temporarily. But Seattle television news anchors nearly wet their pants at the prospect of a Rainier "geological event," and those weren't the only stains: Traces of the mudflow lingered on canyon walls for quite some time, serving as a healthy reminder of The Mountain's volatility.

Autumn snow frames graceful Comet Falls

That said, things were already getting back to normal on our last visit to this peaceful place. After crossing over upper Christine Falls about 0.3 mile into the hike, the well-worn trail climbs very steeply through the forest; take your time, keep plugging away, and tread carefully along trail portions that skirt the top of Van Trump Canyon, with the creek far below.

At about **1.6** miles, you'll encounter a bridge over Falls Creek, which enters from the right, with a small waterfall above. Stay left on the main trail and cross the bridge; you're almost there. A short distance farther, Comet Falls comes into view on a series of steepening switchbacks. The best views of the entire, 320-foot, graduated falls are from the first several switchbacks. Snap your photos, and then continue another quarter mile to a spur trail that leads left to the base of the falls—close enough to wash your grimy face in the mist. Watch your step around the wet area below the falls.

Comet Falls is spectacular, but only the first course on this hike. Many hikers continue onward and upward, another steep three-quarter mile of switchbacks to the top of the falls and through increasingly wildflower-rich meadows. At **2.6** miles, you'll find a junction with a poorly maintained spur trail that leads just over a third of a mile north (right) through Van Trump Park to a grand viewpoint at about 5,800 feet. Bring your wildflower identification guide. A quiz will be given on the way home.

Going Farther

If it's late in the summer, the weather is good, and the footlog over Van Trump Creek just beyond the trail junction at 2.6 miles is in place (it often washes out), you can gain an even better mountain view. From the junction, continue a half mile south on the main trail and then take a spur trail north (right) another very steep half mile to Mildred Point. The end of the trail, 5,800 feet, is a magical spot, with stunning mountain views, an up-close look at the volatile Kautz Glacier, bountiful wildflowers, and, if you're lucky, herds of deer and klatches of mountain goats on nearby cliffs.

If you have two cars or arrange for a drop-off, you can hike one-way out to Longmire for a total of 7.3 miles excluding spur trails. To do so from Van Trump Park, continue about 4.5 miles south down Rampart Ridge via the Van Trump Park and Wonderland Trails (Hike 4). ■

SOUTHWEST FOOTHILLS

7. Round Pass

RATING	DISTANCE	HIKING TIME
★ ★ ★ ★ ☆	7.0 miles round-trip	3.5 hours

ELEVATION GAIN	HIGH POINT	DIFFICULTY	♿
675 feet	3,550 feet	♦ ♦ ♦ ♦ ♦	Yes (ON WEST SIDE ROAD)

TRAIL ACCESSIBLE—UNLESS SNOW LEVEL IS BELOW 2,000 FEET
Jan Feb Mar Apr May Jun Jul Aug Sep Oct Nov Dec

The Hike
Walk (or ride your mountain bike) up a gentle road to trailheads leading to the wild, remote side of the big mountain.

Getting There
From the park's Nisqually Entrance on Highway 706, drive 1 mile up the Longmire-Paradise Road and turn left onto the West Side Road. Follow the West Side Road 3.3 miles to the spot where a locked cable gate closes the road to the public, elevation 2,875 feet. A large parking area is located just south of the gate.

The Trail
Though in excellent condition and driven often by park staff, the West Side Road is closed to the public because of safety concerns. Park officials say mudflows and floods so frequently spit from the South

PERMITS/CONTACT
Entrance fee; no day-hiking passes required/
Longmire Wilderness Information Center, (360) 569-6650

MAPS
Green Trails No. 269, Mount Rainier West; USGS Mount Wow

TRAIL NOTES
Bikes okay; kid-friendly

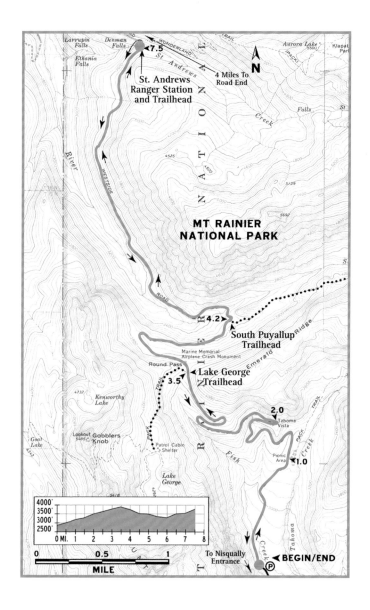

Larrupin
Falls

Denman
Falls

WONDERLAND

Ethania
Falls

‹7.5

St Andrews

4 Miles To
Road End

St. Andrews
Ranger Station
and Trailhead

TRAIL

Aurora Lake

Klapat
Park

N

NATIONAL

Creek

Falls

St

River

WESTSIDE

4525

5135

5697

MT RAINIER
NATIONAL PARK

ROAD

R

‹4.2›

South Puyallup
Trailhead

Emerald

Ridge

Marine Memorial
Airplane Crash Monument

Round Pass

‹Lake George

3.5   ›Trailhead

Kenworthy
Lake

4732

T

PACK

2.0

Tahoma
Vista

R

Goat
Lake

4753

Lookout Gobblers
5485 Knob

Patrol Cabin
Shelter

Fish

Picnic
Area

‹1.0

PACK

TRAIL

Creek

A

Lake
George

5418

I

4000'
3500'
3000'
2500'

0 MI.   1   2   3   4   5   6   7   8

0   0.5   1

MILE

To Nisqually
Entrance

L

Tahoma

Creek

‹BEGIN/END

P

Floods along Tahoma Creek have created views of the mountain along the West Side Road

Tahoma Glacier that there is a danger of private vehicles and their passengers being trapped on the wrong side of a washout. But here's the good news about the West Side Road:

- You can ride a mountain or other suitable gravel bike on the road for at least 7.5 miles, one-way, to trails that climb into alpine meadows of stunning beauty.

- In winter, the road is gated just beyond its intersection with the Longmire-Paradise Road. When the snow level is below 2,000 feet, the West Side Road is an excellent family snowshoe or cross-country ski outing. When the snow level is higher, it would be difficult to find a quieter, more scenic winter walk.

The road climbs gently from the gate, first crossing a huge culvert and quarter-mile-long section of road built in 2000, after Fish Creek carved a new canyon down the middle of the old road. Just beyond is a spectacular view of Mount Rainier and the Sunset Amphitheater, courtesy of the last tree-killing flood and mudflow from the South Tahoma Glacier. Burn pixels here, because if Round Pass is your destination, this is the only photo opportunity of the mountain you'll get.

The road continues to climb gently past a picnic area 1.0 mile from the parking area. This was the site of an old auto campground and trailhead to Emerald Ridge and Indian Henry's Hunting Ground. The way now switches back and begins climbing only slightly more steeply to Tahoma Vista, 2.0 miles from the trailhead. Today, Tahoma Vista fails to live up to its name because the forest has grown and obliterated the view of Rainier.

Continue climbing along the road past two more switchbacks to a huge parking area and turnaround spot at the Lake George trailhead, 3.5 miles from the parking area. You can walk another tenth of a mile on the road to view the Marine Memorial Airplane Crash Monument.

Going Farther

Hikers seeking a longer walk can follow the Lake George Trail (Hike 8) another mile to the lake, or continue hiking the road another 0.7 mile to the South Puyallup trailhead, which leads to St. Andrews Park in a very steep 4.8 miles.

Strong, fast hikers and mountain bikers can continue past the South Puyallup trailhead for another 3.3 miles to the St. Andrews Ranger Station and trailhead. The St. Andrews Trail leads uphill to splendid Klapatche Park in 2.6 steep miles. Hikers bound for Klapatche Park would therefore hike 15 miles round-trip on the road, plus 5.2 miles on backcountry trail for a long, exhausting day hike of 20.2 miles, round-trip.

Bicyclists can continue on the road another 2 miles beyond the ranger station to Klapatche Point, where the road was closed decades ago. The road originally continued 2 miles beyond Klapatche Point to the North Puyallup River, where a beautiful old stone bridge crosses the river to an auto campground. The last 2 miles of the abandoned road make a great spot to pick thimbleberries in the early autumn. ■

8. Lake George

RATING	DISTANCE	HIKING TIME	
★★★ ☆ ☆	8.6 miles round-trip	4.0 hours	
ELEVATION GAIN	HIGH POINT	DIFFICULTY	♿
1,425 feet	4,300 feet	♦ ♦ ◇ ◇ ◇	No
TRAIL ACCESSIBLE			
~~Jan~~ ~~Feb~~ ~~Mar~~ ~~Apr~~ ~~May~~ Jun Jul Aug Sep Oct ~~Nov~~ ~~Dec~~			

The Hike

Climb along a gentle road to a slightly steeper 1-mile trail leading to a clear subalpine lake. Further possibilities include a steep climb to a spectacular view of Rainier at Gobbler's Knob or a 9-mile one-way hike past Goat Lake to a trailhead outside the park at the end of Forest Road 59.

Note: As of 2024, National Forest Service Road 59 (FR 59) is closed temporarily due to multiple washouts that also damaged the Glacier View trailhead. Estimated timeline for repair and reopening is fall 2025 or summer 2026. Check with the Cowlitz Valley Ranger District office for current road status.

Getting There

From the park's Nisqually Entrance on Highway 706, drive 1 mile up the Longmire-Paradise Road and turn left onto the West Side Road. Follow the West Side Road 3.3 miles to the spot where a locked

PERMITS/CONTACT
Entrance fee; no day-hiking passes required/
Longmire Wilderness Information Center, (360) 569-6650

MAPS
Green Trails No. 269, Mount Rainier West; USGS Mount Wow

TRAIL NOTES
Bikes okay on road; kid-friendly

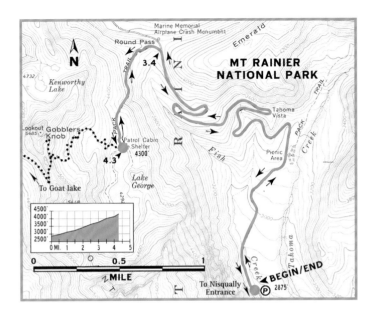

cable gate closes the road to the public, elevation 2,875 feet. A large parking area is located just south of the gate.

The Trail

The first 3.5 miles of this hike follow the West Side Road to Round Pass, described in Hike 7. Leashed pets and mountain bikes are welcome on the West Side Road to Round Pass, but are prohibited on the backcountry trail leading to Lake George. There's a rack at the Lake George trailhead, 3,550 feet above sea level, where you can lock your bike.

The trail climbs gently through forest for 0.9 mile to the lake. There's a patrol cabin above the shore at the northeast end of the lake and a way trail leads around the west shore. Lake George is probably a good turnaround for families with younger children.

Going Farther

It's another 1.2 miles from Lake George to Gobbler's Knob, a lookout site with an up-close-and-personal view of the west side of Rainier. You must work for the view, however, because the trail climbs 1,200 feet in that mile. If you are training for Mount Everest, that shouldn't be a problem.

Here is another option for hikers who have cars parked at the West Side Road and Goat Lake trailheads (Hike 9): Hike from either direction and meet at Gobbler's Knob for a picnic and car-key trade. The Goat Lake Trail junction is 0.2 mile below the summit of Gobbler's Knob. The Goat Lake trailhead is 3.3 miles from that junction. Heaven help the lunkhead who forgets to trade car keys. Unless you want the tougher workout and longer climb, start the one-way hike from the Goat Lake trailhead, which begins almost 2,000 feet higher than the West Side Road trailhead. ■

9. Goat Lake

RATING	DISTANCE	HIKING TIME
★★★★☆	5.0 miles round-trip	2.5 hours

ELEVATION GAIN	HIGH POINT	DIFFICULTY	♿
300 feet	4,600 feet	♦♦♦♦♦	No

TRAIL ACCESSIBLE											
Jan	Feb	Mar	Apr	May	Jun	Jul	Aug	Sep	Oct	Nov	Dec

The Hike

Take the entire family on this hike through flower-filled meadows to a clear alpine lake, with an optional climb to a lookout site with a box seat on Rainier's 50-yard line.

Getting There

Follow Highway 706 east from Ashford for 3.1 miles to Forest Road 59, on the left. You'll see a Mount Tahoma Trail Association access

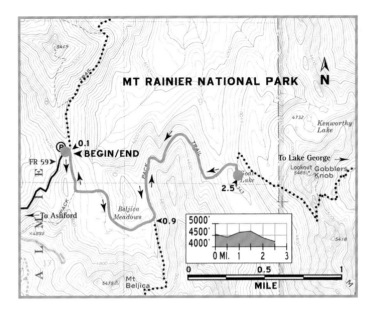

sign near the junction. Turn left on FR 59 and follow it 9 miles up and over a pass with a spectacular view of Rainier, to the gated road closure and trailhead, elevation 4,400 feet. Note: As of 2024, National Forest Service Road 59 (FR 59) is closed temporarily due to multiple washouts that also damaged the Glacier View trailhead. Estimated

PERMITS/CONTACT
USFS Northwest Forest Pass required; free USFS Wilderness Permit at trailhead/ Cowlitz Valley Ranger District, (360) 497-1100

MAPS
Green Trails No. 269, Mount Rainier West; USGS Mount Wow

TRAIL NOTES
Leashed dogs okay; kid-friendly

timeline for repair and reopening is fall 2025 or summer 2026. Check with the Cowlitz Valley Ranger District office for current road status.

The Trail

For the first 0.1 mile, you'll share the trail with hikers bound for Glacier View (Hike 10), climbing to a junction with the Goat Lake Trail (Trail No. 248) at the crest of a 4,500-foot ridge with great peekaboo views of Rainier to the east. Turn right and follow Trail No. 248 as it meanders south along the crest of the ridge before descending 120 feet into Beljica Meadows.

If you've hiked in the summer, you'll soon discover why autumn might be the best time for this hike. There are enough mosquitoes and biting flies in the meadows and around Goat Lake to suck the South Seattle Blood Bank dry, but the poor little critters are all shivering so hard by mid-September they couldn't hit an artery with a ballistic missile.

Turn left 0.9 mile from the trailhead, at the junction with the Christine Lake Trail (Trail No. 249). The trail contours around a ridge to the north, eventually climbing in about a half mile to the high point of the hike. You'll then begin a descent, rounding a second ridge before dropping down to Goat Lake at 4,343 feet. Thus, the major part of the elevation gained on this hike is on the return trip.

Going Farther

Hikers looking for a great view of Rainier face a very strenuous climb of 850 feet in less than a mile to a 5,200-foot saddle just south of the Gobbler's Knob lookout site in Mount Rainier National Park. The trail drops slightly to a junction with the Lake George Trail, 1 mile from Goat Lake, and then climbs steeply to the lookout site. A one-way hike from Goat Lake to the West Side Road trailhead is described in Lake George (Hike 8). ∎

10. Glacier View

RATING	DISTANCE	HIKING TIME	
★★★★☆	5.8 miles round-trip	3.0 hours	
ELEVATION GAIN	HIGH POINT	DIFFICULTY	𝕏
1,000 feet	5,450 feet	◆◆◇◇◇	No
	TRAIL ACCESSIBLE		
	Jan Feb Mar Apr May Jun **Jul Aug Sep Oct** Nov Dec		

The Hike

Walk along a forested ridge with peekaboo views of Rainier to the east and Mount St. Helens to the southwest. End at the airy, rocky site of a fire lookout with an unbeatable view of the west face of Tahoma.

Getting There

Follow Highway 706 east from Ashford for 3.1 miles to Forest Road 59, on the left. You'll see a Mount Tahoma Trail Association access sign near the junction. Turn left on FR 59 and follow it 9 miles up and over a pass with a spectacular view of Rainier to the gated road closure and trailhead, elevation 4,400 feet. Note: As of 2024, National Forest Service Road 59 (FR 59) is closed temporarily due to multiple washouts that also damaged the Glacier View trailhead. Estimated timeline for repair and reopening is fall 2025 or summer 2026. Check with the Cowlitz Valley Ranger District office for current road status.

PERMITS/CONTACT
USFS Northwest Forest Pass required; free USFS Wilderness Permit at trailhead/ Cowlitz Valley Ranger District, (360) 497-1100

MAPS
Green Trails No. 269, Mount Rainier West; USGS Mount Wow

TRAIL NOTES
Leashed dogs okay; kid-friendly

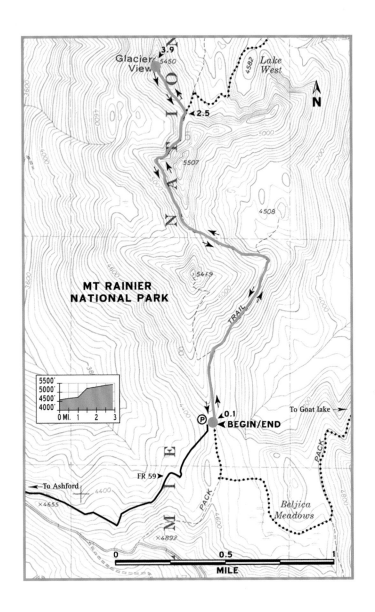

Glacier View
3.9
5450
Lake West
5582

2.5

5507

4508

MT RAINIER
NATIONAL PARK

5419

TRAIL

5500'
5000'
4500'
4000'
0 MI.   1   2   3

To Goat lake →

0.1
BEGIN/END

FR 59 ►

← To Ashford

×4655

PACK

Beljica
Meadows

PACK

×4892

0   0.5   1
MILE

The Trail

This hike begins in the shade of an old forest, where you'll climb 100 feet in less than 0.1 mile to a trail junction on the ridge crest. Turn left here, on Trail No. 267, and follow it as it climbs into the sunshine of a logged area on the ridge's west side.

At **0.5** mile, you'll find an opening in the forest that frames Rainier between silver snags and likely wonder whether the view can get any better at Glacier View, your destination. It can't—but you're out here to put some miles on the old Vibrams, right? Continue climbing a gentle grade as the trail traverses to the east around a 5,600-foot peak and angles west back to a forested saddle, traversing under a second 5,500-foot peak. Look southwest through openings in the trees for a view of Mount St. Helens.

The trail alternately traverses steep meadows, hillside forest, and under cliffs. At **2.2** miles, you'll cross a ridge and begin descending to a saddle and trail junction at **2.6** miles. Turn left here and climb the steepest section of the trail for 0.3 mile to the old lookout site.

A flat campsite to the right of the trail, just short of the open rock summit, might be the best picnic spot. The features on Rainier best seen from here include the Sunset Amphitheater, Tahoma and Puyallup Glaciers, and Success Cleaver. The trail ends on the summit rock, unless you've brought your hang glider.

Lilies are common midsummer trail companions around Mount Rainier

Going Farther

On a hot summer day, the cold waters of Lake West might make a refreshing stop. Return 0.3 mile to the trail junction and turn left. The trail drops steeply for 0.1 mile to a junction with the Lake Helen Trail. Keep right, here, and continue the steep 600-foot descent to the lake, another 0.7 mile. ∎

11. High Rock Lookout

RATING	DISTANCE	HIKING TIME
★★★☆☆	3.2 miles round-trip	1.5 hours

ELEVATION GAIN	HIGH POINT	DIFFICULTY	♿
1,350 feet	5,658 feet	♦♦♦♦◇	No

TRAIL ACCESSIBLE											
Jan	Feb	Mar	Apr	May	Jun	Jul	Aug	Sep	Oct	Nov	Dec

The Hike

A moderately strenuous climb brings you to an awesome cliff-dwelling fire lookout with a view of all of the big snow giants of the South and Central Cascades. There is probably no finer view of the southwest face of Mount Rainier anywhere outside of the national park.

PERMITS/CONTACT
USFS Northwest Forest Pass required/
Cowlitz Valley Ranger District, (360) 497-1100

MAPS
Green Trails No. 301, Randle; USGS Sawtooth Ridge

TRAIL NOTES
Leashed dogs okay; kid-friendly—if they're not afraid of heights; no bikes

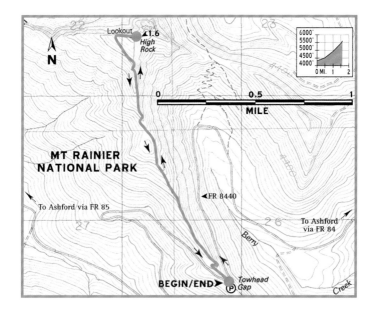

Getting There

Follow Highway 706 east from Ashford 2.3 miles to its junction with Kernihan Road, on the right. Turn right and follow Kernihan Road across the Nisqually River, and at 1.3 miles follow the road as it curves to the left to become Skate Creek Road (Forest Road 52).

Follow Skate Creek Road for 4.7 miles to its junction with Forest Road 84. Turn right on FR 84 and follow it for 6.8 miles to its junction with Forest Road 8440. Turn right on FR 8440 and follow it 2.6 miles to Towhead Gap and the trailhead, elevation 4,300 feet.

The Trail

Nervous about heights? Get that knee-knock sensation when you're on an exposed ridgeline? Don't like looking down and seeing the next patch of earth a loooong ways below? Consider sitting this one out. The rest of you, c'mon up.

What you might have heard about High Rock Lookout trail is true: The final stretch of the trail, approaching the whiteboard-clad lookout—which, you hope, is bolted firmly into the rock, the way it perches precariously here—drops about 500 feet on either side of the ridgeline upon which you stride. Needless to say, it's not a place to let kids scamper about unattended. The final scramble to the top is exposed and intimidating.

But for those who can gulp and proceed, the payoffs are immense: Northward views across the Nisqually Valley to the south face of Rainier are mesmerizing and perhaps unequaled in this area. And spinning around southward grants views of Mount St. Helens, and on clear days, Mount Adams and Mount Hood beyond.

Before you leave for the trail, fill up your water bottles—there's no source up there. And, if you're smart, pack some bug dope. The path itself (look for Trail 266) is short and fairly steep, climbing first up and then along a ridge leading to the lookout. After a short walk through the woods, the trail at just short of one mile climbs out of the trees and into the views. You'll turn briefly to the northwest and then, gaining a ridgeline, scramble up the 0.1 mile, on open rock, to the old storm-battered lookout.

Not surprisingly, the lookout is a favored hangout of people with big lenses and tripods. Photo opportunities are best early in the morning or late in the evening. Just be careful going up or down if it's not full daylight. And remember: Save this one for a clear day. There's not much to see up here if it's socked in. ■

PARADISE AREA

---

12. Nisqually Vista

RATING	DISTANCE	HIKING TIME	
★ ★ ★ ★ ★	1.2-mile loop	30 minutes–1.0 hour	
ELEVATION GAIN	HIGH POINT	DIFFICULTY	♿
200 feet	5,420 feet	◆ ◆ ◆ ◆ ◆	Yes
	TRAIL ACCESSIBLE		
	Jan Feb Mar Apr May Jun **Jul Aug Sep Oct** Nov Dec		

The Hike

Stroll along a pleasant nature trail through the sublime alpine wild-flower meadows near Jackson Visitor Center at Paradise.

Getting There

From the park's Nisqually Entrance on Highway 706, proceed 18 miles on Longmire-Paradise Road to the main Paradise parking area, elevation 5,400 feet. The path begins in the parking loop at the west side of the Paradise parking area (to your immediate left as you enter the Paradise area). It can be reached from the new Henry M. Jackson Memorial Visitor Center in the main parking area by following the main path up the granite steps and turning left (west) at trail junctions until you reach the marked Nisqually Vista Trail.

The Trail

If, heaven forbid, you only have a half hour to spend at Mount Rainier before that Grayline bus—or your nephew's RV—pulls out, this is

---

PERMITS/CONTACT
Entrance fee; no day-hiking passes required/
Paradise Visitor Center, (360) 569-6571

MAPS
Green Trails No. 270S, Paradise; USGS Mount Rainier East

TRAIL NOTES
No dogs; very kid-friendly; no bikes

probably the place to spend it. Nisqually Vista is a rolling, paved nature path that drops gently through splendid wildflower meadows to picture-postcard views of Rainier and the Nisqually Glacier, which lies literally at your feet from a viewpoint at the far end of the loop. It's an easy—although by no means flat—walk through meadows that burst into purple, white, red, yellow, and otherworldly scarlet when lupine, various lilies, aster, heather, bistort, and paintbrush bloom, usually from mid-July through mid-August (the latter part of that time window being more reliable for Paradise). Even to lifelong Rainier hoofers, this is a stunning sight, and if you're here on a bright and preferably (for photography purposes) overcast day, there may be no better—certainly no more easily accessible—place on the planet to make wildflower pictures. By all means, bring the tripod.

Grab an interpretive brochure from the kiosk at the beginning of the trail and head down the hill through a fine forest of hemlock and subalpine fir, to a grand view of Rainier through the gnarled trees. You'll drop down the hill and enter a meadow with a small trickler of a stream. Stay right at the trail junction (you'll come out on the left fork on your return) for the best, in-your-face approach to Rainier.

The Nisqually Vista Trail is the perfect one-stop Rainier hiking experience

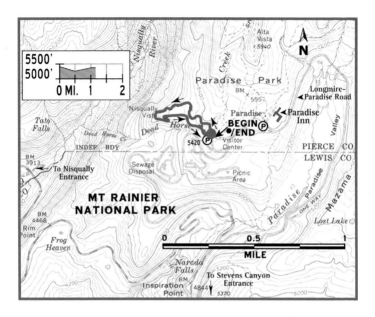

At the center of the meadow is a small pond, Fairy Pool. In season, look close around its edges for shooting star, one of Rainier's most delicate and beautiful wildflowers. The glacier overlook is a quarter mile ahead. Spend some time at the vista and take it all in: The Nisqually Glacier looks docile from here, but it's huge and powerful. Linger long enough, and you're likely to hear it thrash and groan. The Nisqually is very active; it's been alternately creeping forward and retreating by feet and sometimes yards in recent years.

On the loop back, take in grand views of the Tatoosh Range and more lovely flower slopes. Keep your eyes peeled for blacktail deer, grouse, and other critters. Note that park naturalists offer guided walks on this trail, which received some welcomed maintenance in the summer of 2015, at various times in the summer; check at the Jackson Visitor Center information desk for departure times. ∎

13. Alta Vista

RATING	DISTANCE	HIKING TIME	
★ ★ ★ ★	1.6 miles round-trip	1.0 hours	
ELEVATION GAIN	**HIGH POINT**	**DIFFICULTY**	♿
540 feet	5,950 feet	♦ ♦ ♦	No
	TRAIL ACCESSIBLE		
	Jul Aug Sep Oct		

The Hike

A short, sweet, fairly steep ascent to one of the area's premium wildflower-meadow vistas.

Getting There

From the park's Nisqually Entrance on Highway 706, proceed 18 miles on Longmire-Paradise Road to the main Paradise parking area, elevation 5,400 feet. The route described here starts near the Jackson Visitor Center, but the trail can be accessed at various points on other trails in the lower Paradise area.

The Trail

It's a Paradise classic. No other single hike in the park, in fact, gives as quick—and, assuming good weather, as glorious—an introduction to Mother Tahoma than the Alta Vista Trail. Expect plenty of company, but don't worry about the crowds—you'll be transfixed by scenery.

PERMITS/CONTACT
Entrance fee; no day-hiking passes required/
Paradise Visitor Center, (360) 569-6571

MAPS
Green Trails No. 270S, Paradise; USGS Mount Rainier East

TRAIL NOTES
No dogs; kid-friendly—for those who like to climb; no bikes; mostly paved

"... the most luxuriant and the most extravagantly beautiful of all the alpine gardens I ever beheld in all my mountain-top wanderings."
—John Muir, conservationist, 1889

Many Paradise trails begin with the words of a famous former visitor

Like most trails in the Paradise area, this one can be deceiving: It's mostly paved, which tends to create the impression of an easy, nature-trail stroll. But the trail is all up, up, up—and very steep in places. Take your time; there's plenty of flora, fauna, and stunning views to take in, and for most people, it gets easier as you adjust to the altitude (trust us!).

The path climbs up behind the new Jackson Visitor Center, past two trail junctions, and gets thigh-crying steep as you approach a point at about a half mile that marks the bottom of the squashed-circle-shaped Alta Vista "loop." You can hike this loop portion in either direction. To take in the meadow area rising out of Edith Creek, below, take the right fork, which climbs up to a short spur leading to a junction with the Skyline Trail (Hike 14). But if you're already running out of time or gas at the bottom of the loop, take the left fork: It's the more direct (alas, also steeper!) route to Alta Vista summit, elevation 5,940 feet. Here you can turn around and drink in the view of local meadows, the Paradise complex, the knife-ridged Tatoosh Range, and Mounts Adams and St. Helens beyond.

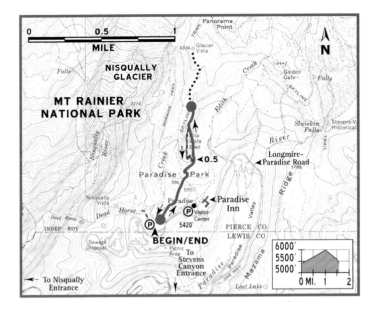

Believe it or not, early Paradise visitors used to take in the same view from their tents—and cars. The old Camp in the Clouds, a car camp, was located near Alta Vista back in Model-T days. Note that you can also get to Alta Vista on a *slightly* less-steep route by turning left on the Skyline Trail about one-third mile from the trailhead and following it up the west side of Alta Vista before dropping down onto the Alta Vista Trail. This route adds only a little in the way of mileage to the hike.

Going Farther

If you're just getting warmed up at Alta Vista and starting to crave that thin air, by all means go where it's thinner: From the top of the Alta Vista Loop, join the Skyline Trail and climb another 0.6 mile and about 400 vertical feet to Glacier Vista, or beyond to Panorama Point on the upper Skyline Loop (Hike 14). ■

Mount Adams and the entire South Cascades are on display from the Upper Skyline Trail above Panorama Point (foreground)

14. Panorama Point/Skyline Loop

RATING	DISTANCE	HIKING TIME
★★★★★	5.5-mile loop	4.0 hours

ELEVATION GAIN	HIGH POINT	DIFFICULTY	♿
1,700 feet	7,100 feet	♦♦♦♦	Yes (TO MYRTLE FALLS VIEWPOINT)

TRAIL ACCESSIBLE
~~Jan Feb Mar Apr May Jun~~ Jul Aug Sep Oct ~~Nov Dec~~

The Hike

One of the highest maintained trails in the park, this challenging, stunning, high-altitude loop whisks you to—and above—all the best scenery at Paradise. It's an annual rite of passage for many Tahoma lovers.

Getting There

From the park's Nisqually Entrance on Highway 706, proceed 18 miles on the Longmire-Paradise Road to the main Paradise parking area, elevation 5,400 feet. The trail starts to the west of the Paradise Ranger Station.

The Trail

On a postcard-perfect August day, we ran into a trio of older women from Puyallup up here, perched at 7,100 feet, enjoying a leisurely lunch. Members of a hiking club, they come back to Rainier to test

PERMITS/CONTACT
Entrance fee; no day-hiking passes required/
Paradise Visitor Center, (360) 569-6571

MAPS
Green Trails No. 270S, Paradise; USGS Mount Rainier East

TRAIL NOTES
No dogs; no bikes; not a good hike for inclement weather

The upper stretches of the Skyline Loop are a Paradise-area hiking highlight

their mettle on the Skyline Loop every year. We'll say this about them: If they can do the loop every summer and walk away smiling, they're tough and blessed all at the same time. The Skyline Loop isn't easy, and—unlike most trails at Paradise—isn't paved, at least for the crucial parts. Thus, this isn't a path for beginners—specifically all those people we see up here in sneakers summer after summer. Snow clings to the high portions of the trail well into summer and even into early fall. Sturdy hiking boots with good traction are a must, and trust us: A hiking staff or ice ax will make you feel a lot safer on the upper portions and will feel mighty good to your sore knees on the way down.

You can hike the loop either way, but we prefer a clockwise route, which gets much of the vertical over with at the beginning while you're still fresh. From the Paradise visitor center, follow the main (paved) path up the hill and follow signs to your left for the Skyline Trail, which climbs at a steep pace and skirts to the west (left) of Alta Vista (Hike 13). At about **1.2** miles, you'll come upon a junction with the Glacier Vista Trail. If you want a more up-close view of the

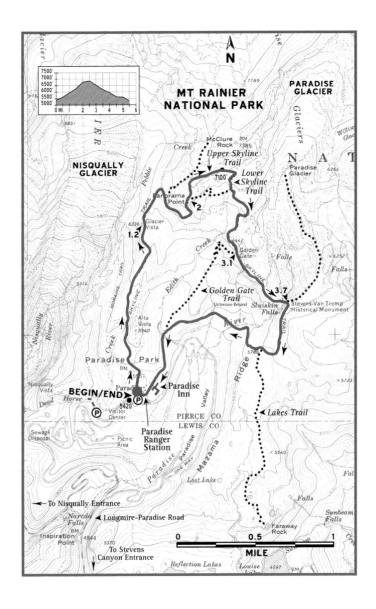

Nisqually Glacier, follow the loop around; it adds only a short distance to the hike. From here, elevation 6,344 feet, continue up into the increasingly rocky, moonscape terrain, climbing at one point on a rocky ledge carved into blocky stone by trail crews.

At about **1.6** miles (6,700 feet), the Pebble Creek Trail exits up and to the left, bound for Camp Muir. Stay right on the Skyline Trail, following signs to Panorama Point, elevation 6,900 feet. From this broad vista, at about **2.0** miles, look south to the world at your feet: the glorious wildflower meadows of Paradise, marmots playing in snowfields, hundreds of hikers forming Gore-Tex ant trails from the parking lot, the stunning Tatoosh Range, and, in the far distance, the Goat Rocks, Mount Adams, and the broken, volcanic crater of Mount St. Helens. You can turn around here for a 4-mile round-trip and take the rest of the week off (if you do, at least take an alternate route, such as Alta Vista, back down); or continue on.

One trail leads due east from Panorama Point across a snowfield. This "Low Skyline" connector is a shortcut, but it's a dangerous, steep snowfield, and rangers have taken to roping it off all summer in recent years. You'll want the better view from above, anyway, so continue upward on the High Skyline Trail, which bypasses the snowfield by switching back 200 feet up a rough-and-tumble rocky slope (note the rather unsightly high-elevation outhouse below the middle switchback; don't knock it until you've sampled the view from the throne!). Come around a large volcanic rock formation, level out at an even more glorious cliff-edge vista, elevation 7,100 feet. Take a rest, get some water, and pat yourself on the tush: It's all downhill from here, cowboy. Look upward from here and see the trail of climbers coming from and going to Camp Muir on the Pebble Creek Trail.

The Skyline Trail drops quickly from here, through more loose rock and late-lingering snow, before coming to more greenery and splendid wildflowers at the Golden Gate Trail junction at **3.1** miles, 6,377 feet. You have a choice here: Bail out and take the Golden Gate Trail back to Paradise, cutting about a mile off the loop, or continue straight on the Skyline Trail. You'll drop another half mile to the Stevens/Van Trump Memorial, where the Paradise Glacier Trail (Hike 18) exits to the left at **3.7** miles. Stay right at this junction and at the next junction with the Lakes Trail along Mazama Ridge, dropping into Paradise Valley and traversing through more wildflowers, past Myrtle Falls, and back to the paved trails around Paradise.

Going Farther

The only way you can go farther from the Skyline Trail is to turn off near the loop's high point and follow the Pebble Creek Trail 0.5 mile to its end at Pebble Creek, a nice lunch spot. Or, commit to some mountaineering by following the climbers' route up the snowfields leading to Camp Muir, the overnight prep camp for Rainier summiteers (Hike 15). ∎

15. Camp Muir

RATING	DISTANCE	HIKING TIME	
★ ★ ★ ★	9.0 miles round-trip	8.0–10.0 hours	
ELEVATION GAIN	HIGH POINT	DIFFICULTY	♿
4,680 feet	10,000 feet	♦ ♦ ♦ ♦ ♦	No
	TRAIL ACCESSIBLE		
	Jan Feb Mar Apr May Jun **Jul Aug Sep** Oct Nov Dec		

The Hike

A grueling, often dangerous alpine ascent from Paradise to Camp Muir, the 10,000-foot primary base camp for Mount Rainier summit expeditions.

Getting There

From the park's Nisqually Entrance on Highway 706, proceed 18 miles on Longmire-Paradise Road to the main Paradise parking area, elevation 5,400 feet. The trail starts to the west of the Paradise Ranger Station.

The Trail

It's a misnomer to call the trek to Camp Muir a "day hike." It's actually an alpine ascent that shouldn't be attempted by people without proper training and gear. We include it here to warn serious hikers to go prepared, and, frankly, to dissuade the inexperienced and ill-equipped from going at all. There's probably no better way to do this than to simply state the facts: people have become stranded and have frozen to death on this route at elevations well below Camp Muir, usually when bad weather appears from nowhere, as it often does on The Mountain.

A whiteout on the route to Muir can prove deadly even to experienced hikers. Even Rainier's backcountry rangers say finding your way down in the fog can be baffling; what you believe to be the natural fall line leading to Paradise actually leads to precipitous cliffs. The only way to be sure you're going the right way is to follow compass headings, and that's difficult with no visible landmarks. Even, clear, cloudless days can prove deadly to hikers without sturdy boots and an ice ax. Most of the upper route is across steep, open snowfields. You've been warned.

That said, for the properly conditioned and equipped (good boots, ice ax, sunscreen!), Muir remains one of the most memorable alpine ascents in Washington. It's about as close as you can get to the summit without roping up and following a guide. The first part of the journey can be made in a variety of ways through the maze of trails in lower Paradise, but most climbers follow the Skyline Trail route described in Hike 14, to its junction with the Pebble Creek Trail, elevation 6,700 feet.

PERMITS/CONTACT
Entrance fee; no day-hiking passes required/
Paradise Visitor Center, (360) 569-6571

MAPS
Green Trails No. 270, Mount Rainier East; USGS Mount Rainier East

TRAIL NOTES
No dogs; no bikes; no fools with tennis shoes and death wishes

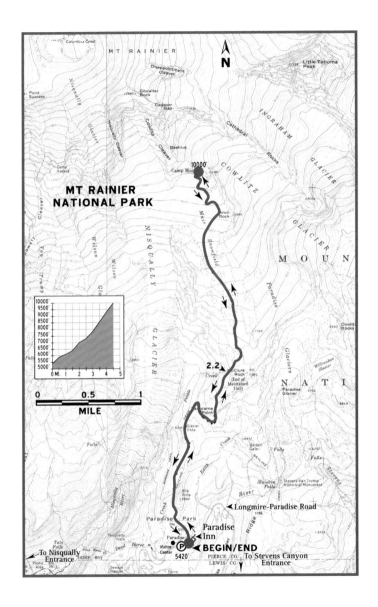

**MT RAINIER
NATIONAL PARK**

N

MT RAINIER

Columbia Crest

Little Tahoma Peak

Disappointment Cleaver

Gibraltar Rock

Point Success

Cadaver Gap

INGRAHAM GLACIER

Camp Hazard

Beehive

Cathedral Rocks

10000'
Camp Muir

COWLITZ

GLACIER

Anvil Rock

NISQUALLY

Main Snowfield

MOUN

Paradise

GLACIER

Cowlitz Rocks

2.2
Clure Rock
[End of Maintained Trail]

Creek

Glacier

Paradise Glacier

Willowbes Glacier

NATI

Falls

Panorama Point

Glacier Vista

Pebble

Creek

Golden Gate

Falls

Falls

Edith

Creek

Sluiskin Falls

Stevens-Van Trump Historical Monument

River

Paradise Park

Ridge

Longmire–Paradise Road

Nisqually Vista

Paradise
**Paradise
Inn**
BEGIN/END

Dead Horse

Visitor Center

5420'

PIERCE CO.
LEWIS CO.

To Nisqually Entrance

To Stevens Canyon Entrance

0   0.5   1
MILE

10000'
9500'
9000'
8500'
8000'
7500'
7000'
6500'
6000'
5500'
5000'
0 MI. 1   2   3   4   5

Hikers pause on the Skyline trail near its junction with the snowfield route to Camp Muir

Here, the path climbs a series of rock steps, leveling off briefly in a half mile at Pebble Creek, a good lunch spot at **2.2** miles.

From this point on, you'll be following cairns, wands, and snow steps upward, over the Muir Snowfield. If the conditions are right, snow is deep, and steps are prekicked, it's an exhausting, albeit fairly safe, ascent. But if the surface is icy, or it's late summer and you see crevasses or surface cracks, bag it and go back. The surface you're standing on might not be safe, and unless you're roped up, you're asking for some very unpleasant crevasse-rescue training.

The climb is long and taxing; nearly 3,000 feet in 2 miles, all on snow. Plan on four hours or so from Pebble Creek. Follow the established trail through the snowfield (stay off the rock; it's fragile and dangerous), past Anvil Rock (9,584 feet) to Camp Muir, where a permanent stone bunkhouse, gear sheds, outhouses, and, typically, a small armada of mountaineering tents, are tucked between rock outcroppings. Climbers rest here for a wee-hours assault on the 14,411-foot summit via the Ingraham Glacier route. The view from the camp is stupendous—all the way to central Oregon on a clear day. ■

16. Paradise to Narada Falls

RATING	DISTANCE	HIKING TIME
★★★	1.6 miles one way	45 minutes
ELEVATION GAIN	**HIGH POINT**	**DIFFICULTY** ♿
900 feet	5,400 feet	♦ No
	TRAIL ACCESSIBLE	
	Jan Feb Mar Apr May **Jun Jul Aug Sep Oct** Nov Dec	

The Hike

This is a pleasant, all-downhill, one-way hike from Paradise through the Paradise River valley, past streamside wildflowers and numerous small waterfalls to a viewpoint overlooking majestic Narada Falls.

Getting There

From the park's Nisqually Entrance on Highway 706, proceed 18 miles on Longmire-Paradise Road to the Paradise parking area, elevation 5,400 feet. Look for the Lakes Trail trailhead at the east side of the parking area, near where the lot funnels into a one-way road through Paradise Valley.

The Trail

For a trail with multiple delights, this route gets surprisingly little use. Most people who spend a day at Paradise naturally focus on the uphill, clogging paved paths through wildflower meadows. You'll probably want to do the same, but don't overlook this fun, refreshingly cool,

PERMITS/CONTACT
Entrance fee; no day-hiking passes required/
Paradise Visitor Center, (360) 569-6571

MAPS
Green Trails No. 270S, Paradise; USGS Mount Rainier East

TRAIL NOTES
No dogs; kid-friendly—it's a winner with them; no bikes

The Paradise River flows gracefully toward Narada Falls

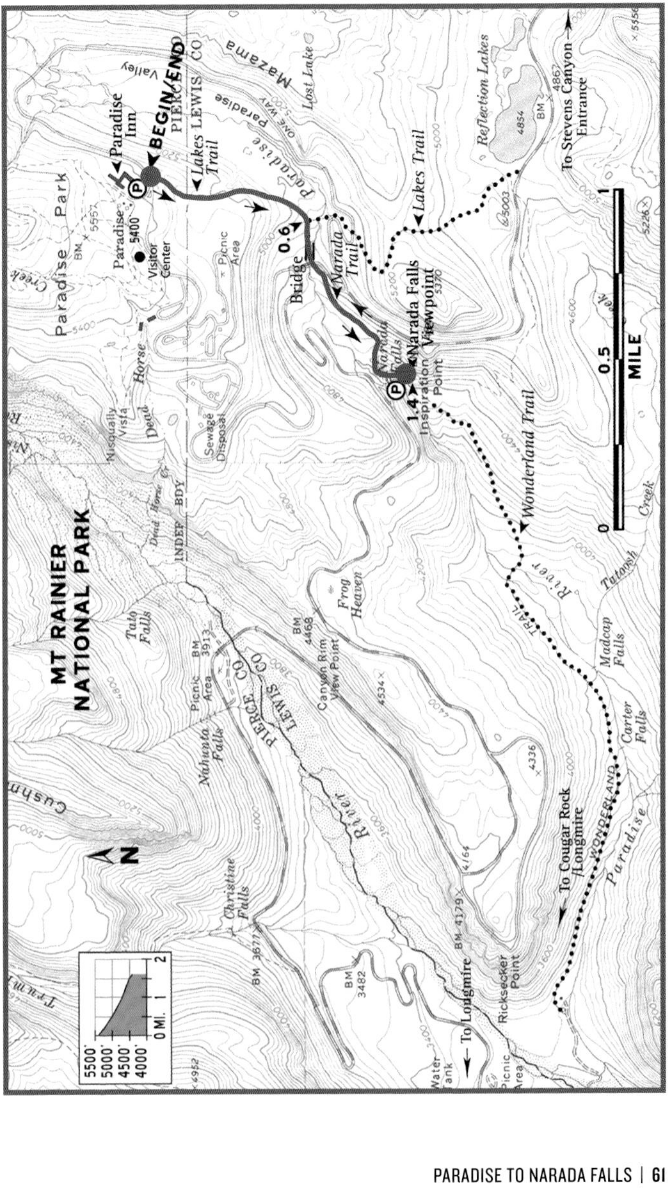
MT RAINIER NATIONAL PARK
BEGIN/END
Paradise Inn
Paradise
Visitor Center
Paradise Park
Lakes Trail
Narada Trail
Bridge
0.6
1.4
Narada Falls Viewpoint
Inspiration Point
Wonderland Trail
Lakes Trail
Reflection Lakes
Lost Lake
Mazama
ONE WAY
To Stevens Canyon Entrance
Frog Heaven
Canyon Rim View Point
Tato Falls
Nahunta Falls
Christine Falls
Madcap Falls
Carter Falls
Ricksecker Point
To Cougar Rock /Longmire
To Longmire
PIERCE CO
LEWIS CO
INDEF BDY
Sewage Disposal
Picnic Area
Nisqually Vista
Dead Horse Cr
River
Paradise
Tatoosh Creek
WONDERLAND TRAIL
0
0.5
1
MILE
N
5500'
5000'
4500'
4000'
0 MI.
1
2

all-downhill walk in the opposite direction: Simply have your companions drop you at the Lakes Trail, and then arrange to meet you down the road at Narada Falls in an hour or so.

The trail drops from Paradise at a pleasant pace through the Paradise Valley, through wildflower-festooned meadows and, soon, cool forests of subalpine fir. At **0.6** mile, the Lakes Trail veers left (southeast) toward Reflection Lakes. Stay right on the Narada Falls Trail, now traveling very close to the gurgling Paradise River, one of the most beautiful streams in the park. Watch for American dippers, also known as water ouzels—small, steel-gray water birds—playing in the froth and bobbing their heads from stone perches. In a short distance, river and trail both meet the Stevens Canyon Road. Cross it, walk east across the bridge, and pick up the trail again on the other side.

From here, the path drops more quickly through cool forest, now on the east bank of the river, to the Narada Falls parking area. Note that during winter months, this same trail, marked by orange wands, is the first portion of a very popular ski and snowshoe route that continues from the Narada Falls parking lot to Reflection Lakes.

The trail ends on a closed road, near a park restroom at the Narada Falls day-use area. But before you cross the bridge to the car, pick up the paved trail across the way and proceed another 0.2 mile downhill to a viewpoint of Narada Falls, one of the most spectacular in the park. Get a picture, then walk back up to the parking area and your waiting ride.

Going Farther

If you're liking what you see, continue downstream from the Narada Falls overlook to a junction with the Wonderland Trail. Go right, toward Longmire, and follow the river just short of a mile to Paradise River Camp, continuing another half mile to Madcap and Carter Falls. From there, you can return uphill to Narada Falls, or continue another mile downhill, crossing the Nisqually River and exiting on the highway at Cougar Rock Campground. You could go even farther by continuing from the campground 1.7 miles on the Wonderland Trail to Longmire (Hike 5). The one-way trip from Paradise to Longmire is about 7 miles, with an elevation drop of 2,800 feet. ■

17. Upper Paradise Valley

RATING	DISTANCE	HIKING TIME
★★★★	1.8 miles round-trip	1.0 hour

ELEVATION GAIN	HIGH POINT	DIFFICULTY	&#9855;
600 feet	5,800 feet	◆◆	No

TRAIL ACCESSIBLE		
Jun Jul Aug Sep Oct		

The Hike

Take a short, quick climb up the gurgling Paradise River from Fourth Crossing on Paradise Valley Road to Rampart Ridge, and sample some of the best views, wildflower meadows, and terrain of the Paradise area—without the crowds.

Heather blooms along the upper Paradise River are a summer highlight

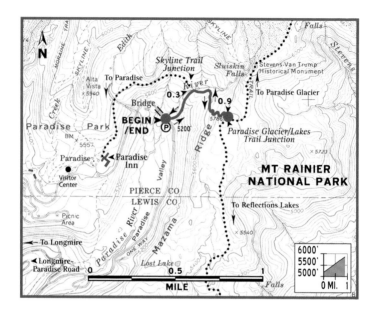

Getting There

From the park's Nisqually Entrance on Highway 706, proceed 18 miles on Longmire-Paradise Road to the main Paradise area. Continue east through the parking lot and drive downhill on the (now one-way) Paradise Valley Road. Continue about 0.75 mile to an unsigned but obvious parking area on the right side of the road, just beyond a stone bridge over the Paradise River, elevation 5,200 feet. The trailhead, marked "Fourth Crossing," is directly across the road, toward The Mountain.

The Trail

It's not listed in most guidebooks. It barely shows up on park maps. So why should you hike it? For those exact reasons. Upper Paradise Valley, shown on most maps as the Fourth Crossing Trail, is a sleeper, a little backdoor entryway into the marvelous, wildflower-and-blue-skies extravaganza known as Paradise. We list it here because if

Hikers traverse a rocky, wildflower-filled bowl below Mazama Ridge

you're like most people, you're probably arriving at Paradise on a sunny Saturday or Sunday afternoon in June, July, or August—only to find a road sign near the main parking lot bearing bad news: "Parking area full. Please proceed." Huh? You figured out how to strap in the kiddy car seat, crated up the dog, and fought traffic for three hours, all for a wildflower drive-by?

PERMITS/CONTACT
Entrance fee; no day-hiking passes required/
Paradise Visitor Center, (360) 569-6571

MAPS
Green Trails No. 270S, Paradise; USGS Mount Rainier East

TRAIL NOTES
Very kid-friendly

Fret not. A little farther down the road, where most people only venture on their way home, is Fourth Crossing, a little-used (at least in summer) connector trail between the highway and the popular Skyline Trail (Hike 14). It follows the Paradise River—up this high, it's not really a river at all, just a delightfully exuberant stream, with plenty of waterfalls—through some of the most spectacular wildflower minimeadows in the park. And here's an added bonus: Unlike most paths departing from the Paradise parking lot, this is a real trail, with actual *dirt*, not asphalt.

The trail is a photographer's delight, offering the rare chance to photograph orange and magenta paintbrush, lupine, aster, red heather, and other wildflowers against the backdrop of rushing whitewater (Tip: cloudy days are best for photos). Watch for American dippers (small, steel-gray water birds) in the foamy water.

If you're riding on old knees, have the kids along, or don't have much time, just walk the first one-third mile up to the junction with the Skyline Trail and head back down. But if you have time, hang a right, proceed into the open bowl, and take the ascending switchbacks another long half mile up to the turnaround point: the three-way junction with the Paradise Glacier and Lakes (Mazama Ridge) Trails. Mountain views from here are sublime.

If they're not quite sublime enough, just keep walking up the Paradise Glacier Trail; eventually Mounts Adams and St. Helens will pop into view.

Going Farther

There are three options for a longer hike. At the first junction with the Skyline Trail, turn left instead of right and proceed about 1.3 miles back to the Paradise parking area, where you can walk the road back to your car for a loop trip of about 2.25 miles. Or, create a longer, in-and-back day hike by following the Paradise Glacier or Lakes Trails from the trail junction at this hike's turnaround point (Hikes 18 and 19). ∎

18. Paradise Glacier

RATING	DISTANCE	HIKING TIME	
★ ★ ★ ★	6.5 miles round-trip	2.5 hours	
ELEVATION GAIN	HIGH POINT	DIFFICULTY	⛷
1,000 feet	6,400 feet	◆ ◆	No
	TRAIL ACCESSIBLE		
	~~Jan Feb Mar Apr May Jun~~ Jul Aug Sep Oct ~~Nov Dec~~		

The Hike

One of the most popular moderate day hikes from Paradise, the Paradise Glacier Trail follows a route pioneered by early Rainier summiteers. It has since been hiked by millions of visitors who hoofed it up here to see the fabulous (and now mostly vanished) Paradise Ice Caves.

Getting There

From the park's Nisqually Entrance on Highway 706, proceed 18 miles on Longmire-Paradise Road to the Paradise parking area, elevation 5,400 feet. Look for the Skyline Trail trailhead next to the Paradise Inn, but be aware that several trails in the main Paradise complex lead to the Skyline Trail. If the Paradise parking area is full, this hike can be started from the Fourth Crossing trailhead, 0.75 mile east of Paradise on Paradise Valley Road, where parking is usually available (Hike 17).

PERMITS/CONTACT
Entrance fee; no day-hiking passes required/
Paradise Visitor Center, (360) 569-6571

MAPS
Green Trails No. 270S, Paradise; USGS Mount Rainier East

TRAIL NOTES
No dogs; kid-friendly—for the older and stronger ones; no bikes

The Trail

More than a few old ghosts linger along this route. The Paradise Glacier Trail is actually an extension of one leg of the popular Skyline Loop (Hike 14) to a permanent snowfield high on Mount Rainier. The trail roughly follows the route chosen by early mountaineers Hazard Stevens and Philemon Van Trump, the climbers widely credited with The Mountain's first official ascent in 1870 (whether they were the first to the "true" summit is a matter of continuing debate). In midsummer, stunning fields of lilies, lupine, paintbrush, heather, bear grass, and other wildflowers blanket slopes above and below the path. Views of surrounding peaks are spectacular.

From the main Paradise trail complex, follow any of the myriad paths east to the Skyline Trail, rising steadily to a nice photo opportunity at Myrtle Falls in 0.4 mile. Then traverse gently about 300 feet downhill to the Paradise River and the Fourth Crossing Trail junction (see Hike 17). From here, the path climbs gentle switchbacks to the top of Mazama Ridge and a junction with the Lakes (Mazama Ridge) Trail at about **1.4** miles. Stay left (north) and follow the ridgeline up, checking your rear-view mirror for views of Mount Adams, until you come upon the large stone monument to the aforementioned Stevens and Van Trump (as well as their native guide, Sluiskin), who reportedly parked their base camp here, about 2.0 miles from where you parked your Lincoln Navigator.

The Skyline Trail joins near here; stay right and head up through the moonscape-like, dusty terrain typical of Rainier above 6,000 feet. You'll follow an old moraine of the Paradise Glacier for about a mile through barren and exposed terrain—beware bad weather here—to the glacier itself, now essentially a permanent snowfield quite popular with early- and late-season backcountry skiers and snowboarders.

Cairn markers still lead the way to the former site of the Paradise Ice Caves, one of Rainier's leading attractions until glacial retreat claimed them. Some wind-carved ice caves do still present themselves here on occasion: Don't enter them unless you know what you're doing, which most of us don't. The view behind you of Mount

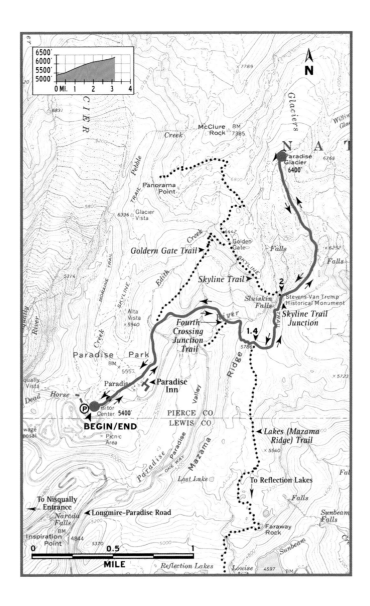

Wildflowers and views of the Tatoosh Range are highlights of the Paradise Glacier Trail

Adams, Mount St. Helens, the Goat Rocks, and the Tatoosh Range is reward enough for this climb.

Note: Upper portions of the trail remain snow covered until late summer; wear sturdy hiking boots and stay on the marked trail.

Going Farther

You can return to Paradise via the Skyline (Hike 14) or Golden Gate Trails for a longer hike with more elevation gain. ■

19. High Lakes Loop

RATING	DISTANCE	HIKING TIME
★ ★ ★ ★	3.0-mile loop	2.0 hours

ELEVATION GAIN	HIGH POINT	DIFFICULTY	♿
600 feet	5,500 feet	♦ ♦	No

TRAIL ACCESSIBLE
Jan Feb Mar Apr May **Jun Jul Aug Sep Oct** Nov Dec

The Hike
A short, pleasant, moderate loop with great views, ample wild-flowers, and abundant wildlife takes you by the shores of gorgeous alpine lakes.

Getting There
From the park's Nisqually Entrance on Highway 706, proceed 15.6 miles on Longmire-Paradise Road to the Stevens Canyon turn-off. Turn right and follow Stevens Canyon Road 1.7 miles to the long parking area along Reflection Lakes, elevation 4,865 feet. The loop begins on the Wonderland Trail at either end of the parking lot.

The Trail
Here's a grand way to sample all the alpine delights of the Paradise area without fighting the Paradise crowds. Make no mistake: Reflection Lakes is probably number two on Rainier's day-use hit

PERMITS/CONTACT
Entrance fee; no day-hiking passes required/
Paradise Visitor Center, (360) 569-6571

MAPS
Green Trails No. 270S, Paradise; USGS Mount Rainier East

TRAIL NOTES
No dogs; kid-friendly—for the stronger ones; no bikes

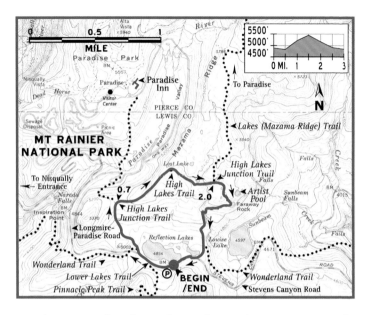

parade, so you still might need to get here early on a summer week-end. But once you're out of the parking lot, you're not liable to run into nearly as many gapers from Nebraska out for a day on the trail.

You can walk this loop, which combines three separate trails, in either direction (and you can walk a longer version of it from Paradise; see "Going Farther" on page 70). But we like to start on the west side of the parking lot, hiking in a clockwise direction and saving the big view from Faraway Rock for the end.

Begin on the Wonderland Trail (mileages indicated here are from the center of the parking lot). In a short distance, go right on the Lakes Trail and head up through a wet, meadowy area to a junction with the High Lakes Trail at **0.75** mile and 5,100 feet. Turn right (east) and traverse about 1.25 miles across pleasantly flat trail through a mixed forested area, with occasional views of Rainier and the Tatoosh Range, to a junction with the Lakes (Mazama Ridge) Trail at **2.0** miles and 5,300 feet. Turn right, and head back downhill, stopping for a

Aptly named Reflection Lake greets hikers completing the High Lakes Loop

look at Artist Pool (a small tarn) and then at Faraway Rock to take in the precipitous, cliff-edge view of Lake Louise, Reflection Lakes, the Tatoosh Range, and much of Stevens Canyon. Stay away from the edge: It's about 500 feet down.

The trail back down to the car is gorgeous, with ample wildflowers and wild huckleberries in season. Keep your eyes peeled for blacktail deer or even a rare black bear. At about **2.6** miles, meet up again with the Wonderland Trail. Stay right and follow it a short distance back to the parking area.

Going Farther
You can make a loop of about 6 miles by hiking the Lakes Trail north from Reflection Lakes all the way up Mazama Ridge to the Skyline Trail, walking east to Paradise, and then south back to Reflection Lakes via the western portion of the Lakes Trail. ∎

20. Pinnacle Saddle

RATING ★★★★	DISTANCE 2.6 miles round-trip	HIKING TIME 2.0 hours	
ELEVATION GAIN 1,055 feet	HIGH POINT 5,920 feet	DIFFICULTY ♦ ♦ ♦	♿ No
	TRAIL ACCESSIBLE Jan Feb Mar Apr May Jun **Jul Aug Sep Oct** Nov Dec		

The Hike
On clear days, this is a delightful, view-rich ascent from Reflection Lakes. Climb through subalpine forest into open, rocky terrain to a grand vista of Rainier from the saddle between Pinnacle and Plummer Peaks, two crown jewels of the Tatoosh Range.

Getting There
From the park's Nisqually Entrance on Highway 706, proceed 15.6 miles on Longmire-Paradise Road to the Stevens Canyon turnoff.

Fine handiwork of trail crew members paves the way for Pinnacle Saddle hikers

Turn right and follow Stevens Canyon Road 1.7 miles to the long parking area along Reflection Lakes, elevation 4,865 feet. The trail begins across Stevens Canyon Road from the center of the parking strip.

The Trail

Okay, there has to be one, single *best* view of Rainier from the south side of the park. And this is it. You'll have to sweat a little to get there,

PERMITS/CONTACT
Entrance fee; no day-hiking passes required/
Paradise Visitor Center, (360) 569-6571

MAPS
Green Trails No. 270S, Paradise; USGS Mount Rainier East

TRAIL NOTES
No dogs; kid-friendly—for the stronger ones; no bikes

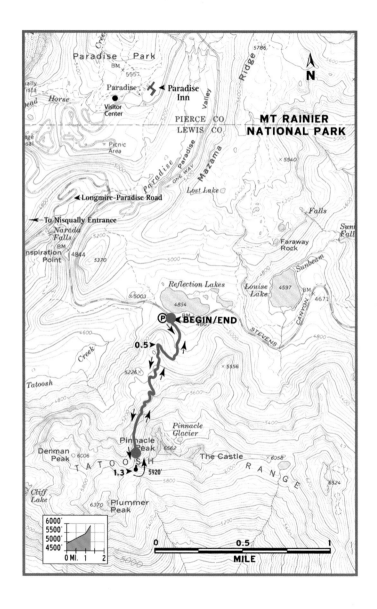

Paradise Park

Paradise

Paradise
Inn

Visitor
Center

Horse

Picnic
Area

PIERCE CO.
LEWIS CO.

MT RAINIER
NATIONAL PARK

Longmire-Paradise Road

To Nisqually Entrance

Narada
Falls

Inspiration
Point

Reflection Lakes

Lost Lake

Falls

Faraway
Rock

Sunbeam

Louise
Lake

Creek

(P) BEGIN/END

0.5

Tatoosh

Pinnacle
Glacier

Denman
Peak

Pinnacle
Peak

TATOOSH

1.3 5920'

The Castle

RANGE

Cliff
Lake

Plummer
Peak

6000'
5500'
5000'
4500'

0 Mi. 1   2

0   0.5   1

MILE

but Pinnacle Saddle is one of the most impressive day hikes in the park—a certified Do Not Miss for lovers of high alpine views.

From the Reflection Lakes parking lot, begin climbing gently through a pleasant forest, with occasional meadows dotted by pink Lewis monkeyflower and other blossoms. At about **0.5** mile, the pace steepens. You'll cross several large boulder fields as views of Rainier, the upper Nisqually drainage, and even faraway Comet Falls begin to open up. Before you know it, you'll be rising above tree line, following a very rocky, consistently steep path through a rubble field below imposing, 6,562-foot Pinnacle Peak. Note the great rock work done over the decades here by trail crews, who have built landscape-perfect rock walls using only available materials and muscle.

It feels like a long **1.3** miles up, but the scene at the top is one of the most dramatic in the park: A narrow gap in the saddle between rocky Pinnacle and Plummer Peaks opens to sweeping views of the South Cascades, from Mount St. Helens to Mount Adams, and the Goat Rocks (themselves the remnants of an ancient, collapsed volcano). Turn around and, if it's clear, prepare to be wowed: Rainier in all her south-face glory is rarely on finer display than from right here.

Note that this is another Rainier trail where sturdy hiking boots are vital. Snow lingers on the upper portions well into the summer, and a hiking staff or ice ax can be of great aid. Also, carry plenty of water. None is available along the route after midsummer.

Going Farther

From the saddle, numerous way trails spread out east and west. The eastern path winds up toward the top of Pinnacle Peak, but quickly deteriorates into an open rock scramble. Proceeding beyond this point without climbing gear and knowledge is a dangerous gamble.

One trail to the west leads along the gorgeous parkland of the saddle to some great lunch spots with sunny, south-facing views; another climbs the ridge toward the top of Plummer Peak, where a small tarn is located. It's a fairly exposed, cliff-top route. ■

21. Bench and Snow Lakes

RATING	DISTANCE	HIKING TIME
★ ★ ★	2.6 miles round-trip	1.5 hours

ELEVATION GAIN	HIGH POINT	DIFFICULTY	♿
700 feet	4,700 feet	♦ ♦	No

	TRAIL ACCESSIBLE	
Jan Feb Mar Apr May Jun	Jul Aug Sep Oct	Nov Dec

The Hike

Enjoy rich views on this hike with plenty of up and downs and a pair of scenic alpine lakes in the shadow of Mount Rainier.

Getting There

From the park's Nisqually Entrance on Highway 706, proceed 15.6 miles on Longmire-Paradise Road to the Stevens Canyon turn-off. Turn right and follow Stevens Canyon Road 3 miles east, past Reflection Lakes and Louise Lake, to a small turnout on the right side of the road, elevation 4,520 feet. Note that the lot only holds about a dozen cars, and often is full in the summer.

The Trail

Don't be fooled by the map. Bench and Snow Lakes, twin alpine beauties in a broad expanse of meadowland with gorgeous displays of summer wildflowers and often-spectacular autumn color, lie at

PERMITS/CONTACT
Entrance fee; no day-hiking passes required/
Paradise Visitor Center, (360) 569-6571

MAPS
Green Trails No. 270S, Paradise; USGS Mount Rainier East

TRAIL NOTES
No dogs; kid-friendly—for the stronger ones; no bikes

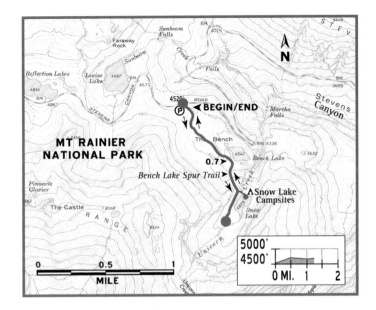

about the same elevation as the trailhead. But you'll do quite a bit of up and down to get there, and on warm summer days the route can be hot, the trail dusty. On the other hand, none of these things ever stopped you before, and the view from Snow Lake makes the trail, the crowds, and even the annoying black flies—which can be atrocious here in midsummer—seem bearable.

From the trailhead along Stevens Canyon Road, the trail climbs quickly up the first ridge, at times on a boardwalk installed over a particularly muddy or dusty area (depending on the weather). As you descend the far side and level out, you'll be walking on "The Bench," a broad plain with open meadows, a few old snags, and killer mountain views. At **0.7** mile, a short spur trail leads down to Bench Lake. Don't waste your time with the steep, unmaintained approach. There's not much to see at the shore, and thickets of scrubby alders and other shrubs prevent you from walking along the lake.

A well-worn path crosses "The Bench" on its way to Snow Lake

Snow Lake is another story. Continue another half mile, crossing a marshy area and then climbing another ridge. The lake, perched in a glacial cirque below 6,935-foot Unicorn Peak, the king of the Tatoosh Range, is a stunner, with deep, turquoise water and a fabulous view of Rainier. Expect snow to linger on the far side of the lake well into the summer. A side trail leads a quarter mile to the left, across Unicorn Creek and down to the lakeshore to two backcountry campsites that look too good to be back and spend a night here. A more memorable view would be hard to find. Remember to save some energy for the trip out: about 300 feet of this hike's elevation gain comes at the end. ■

STEVENS CANYON/
OHANAPECOSH

22. Stevens Creek

RATING	DISTANCE	HIKING TIME	
★★☆☆☆	1.4 miles round-trip	1.0 hour	
ELEVATION GAIN	**HIGH POINT**	**DIFFICULTY**	♿
535 feet	3,100 feet	♦♦♦◇◇	No
	TRAIL ACCESSIBLE		
	Jan Feb Mar Apr May **Jun Jul Aug Sep Oct** Nov Dec		

The Hike
Make a short, steep hike downhill through a mixed forest to a unique waterfall on Stevens Creek.

Getting There
From the park's Stevens Canyon Entrance on Highway 123, drive about 10.8 miles west on Stevens Canyon Road to the Box Canyon Picnic Area (just beyond the tunnel after the Box Canyon Exhibit) on the left (south) side of the road, elevation 3,100 feet. The trail begins on the east side of the parking lot. If you're arriving from the west, the trailhead is about 8.3 miles west of the junction with the Longmire-Paradise Road.

The Trail
Stevens Creek Trail isn't flashy, but it goes someplace pretty special. On first glance, only two things stand out about this little-used

---

PERMITS/CONTACT
Entrance fee; no day-hiking passes required/Ohanapecosh Visitor Center, (360) 569-6581; Longmire Wilderness Information Center, (360) 569-6650

MAPS
Green Trails No. 270, Mount Rainier East; USGS Mount Rainier East

TRAIL NOTES
No dogs; too steep for small kids or creaky knees; no bikes

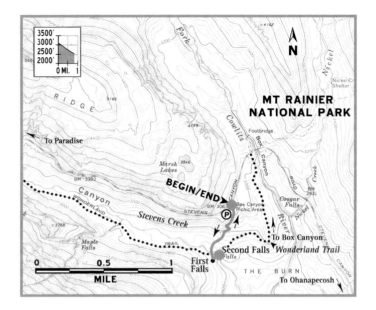

connector between Stevens Canyon Road and the Wonderland Trail, far below in Stevens Canyon: the topography and the decided lack of crowds. Unlike most trails you're likely to hike in Rainier, this one drops down below 3,000 feet, through a fascinating forest of white-barked birch and other deciduous trees. Sword ferns and other greenery dot the forest floor, which is alive with fungi, mushrooms, and other moist-climate plants you'd expect to see in a temperate rain forest or low-lying forest around Puget Sound. It's almost like walking through a terrarium; the forest is peaceful and silent until you reach 0.5 mile, when Stevens Creek becomes audible below.

When the trail reaches the dark, humid canyon floor, you'll find a short spur leading left down to a fenced overlook of a gorgeous, unnamed low-rushing falls on Stevens Creek. A short distance downstream is another falls. Continue on about a tenth of a mile to a junction with the Wonderland Trail and a bridge over Stevens Creek. The stream here is fascinating, filled with large, smooth,

The falls on Stevens Creek is the only sound you're likely to hear on this hike

almost sculpted boulders. If you're like us, you'll be wishing you had more light down here to take photographs—and wishing you hadn't packed that heavy long lens. The trek back up the trail to the car is even worse than you feared on the way down. It's unmercifully steep, but mercifully short.

Going Farther

You can follow the Wonderland Trail from the Stevens Creek Bridge at the end of this hike for an additional 1.2 miles and 400 vertical feet up to the Box Canyon interpretive site on Stevens Canyon Road. The 0.3 mile interpretive trail at Box Canyon, where the Muddy Fork of the Cowlitz River cuts through a deep gorge, is also well worth your time. ■

RATING	DISTANCE	HIKING TIME
★★★★	11.8 miles round-trip	6.5 hours
ELEVATION GAIN	HIGH POINT	DIFFICULTY ♿
2,850 feet	5,900 feet	♦♦♦♦ No

TRAIL ACCESSIBLE
Jan Feb Mar Apr May Jun **Jul Aug Sep Oct** Nov Dec

The Hike

Save this strenuous hike for a clear day to appreciate the spectacular view of Rainier and the green valley of Indian Bar. Strong hikers can continue 1.9 miles to Indian Bar—one of the most scenic backcountry camps in the park—or with a car-key exchange, can continue past Indian Bar to the Summerland trailhead, 15.5 miles one-way.

Getting There

Drive up the Stevens Canyon Road 10 miles from the park's Stevens Canyon Entrance on Highway 123 to the Box Canyon parking area, elevation 3,050 feet. The trailhead is across the road from the parking area, just east of the Box Canyon Nature Trail.

The Trail

One advantage to this serious climb is that the trail is mostly in forest shade. You'll stay relatively cool until you approach the

PERMITS/CONTACT
Entrance fee; no day-hiking passes required/Ohanapecosh Visitor Center, (360) 569-6581; Longmire Wilderness Information Center, (360) 569-6650

MAPS
Green Trails No. 270, Mount Rainier East; USGS Ohanapecosh Hot Springs

TRAIL NOTES
No dogs; not a good choice for kids; no bikes

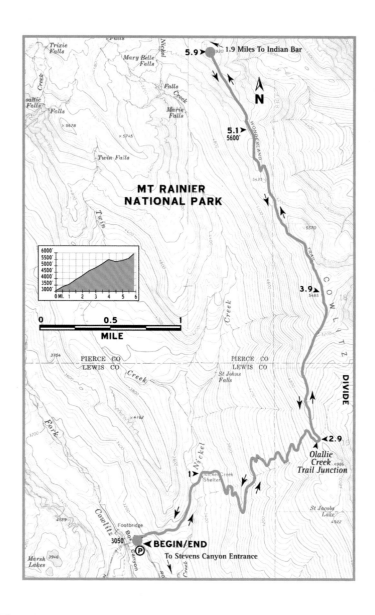

5.9► ⊙ 5930 1.9 Miles To Indian Bar

N

5.1►
5600'

MT RAINIER
NATIONAL PARK

3.9►
5485

◄**2.9**

*Olallie
Creek*
Trail Junction

Nickel Creek
Shelter

◄BEGIN/END
3050' ℗

To Stevens Canyon Entrance

Footbridge

Marsh
Lakes

PIERCE CO
LEWIS CO

PIERCE CO
LEWIS CO

St Johns
Falls

St Jacobs
Lake

Trixie
Falls

Mary Belle
Falls

Falls

Marie
Falls

Twin Falls

saltic
Falls

Falls

6000'
5500'
5000'
4500'
4000'
3500'
3000'
0 Mi. 1 2 3 4 5 6

0   0.5   1
MILE

recommended turnaround spot, a 5,900-foot knoll with a stunning view of The Mountain and of Indian Bar, 800 feet below.

Begin by climbing at a moderate grade to a footlog across Nickel Creek at **1.0** mile. Pass a large group camp on the opposite side of the creek (not readily visible from the main trail since its 2007 relocation). The trail now climbs more steeply, crossing a Nickel Creek tributary only to switch back and recross the creek. The trail climbs steadily in switchbacks for 1.9 miles, gaining more than 1,000 feet, to Cowlitz Divide and a junction with the Olallie Creek Trail at **2.9** miles. Turn left at the junction and follow the Wonderland Trail as it climbs along the crest of Cowlitz Divide.

The trail continues through forest for another mile, climbing steeply at times over the top of a 5,400-foot summit at **3.9** miles. You'll keep climbing through thinning forest past a 5,600-foot peak on the left at **5.1** miles. The way continues up the ridge for another 0.8 mile to a wide knoll, at 5,900 feet and 5.9 miles from the trailhead.

This is a good spot for a picnic and turnaround, with views of Rainier's Ohanapecosh Glacier and Mount Tahoma. In the valley below is the infant Ohanapecosh River and fabled Indian Bar, a splendid alpine campsite and meadow. Take off your boots and let the mountain breezes cool those barking dogs.

Going Farther

From this point, the trail drops steeply into the valley, arriving at Indian Bar 7.8 miles from the trailhead. Strong hikers willing to climb the 800 vertical feet back up from Indian Bar will find the scenery well worth the extra 1.9 miles. The valley is wide and flat, wildflowers abound, and few places around the park are so well-suited for hanging out in the sunshine.

An option for marathon day hikers with cars parked at both the Box Canyon and Summerland trailheads (Hike 33) is a one-way hike and key exchange at Indian Bar, about halfway on the 15.5-mile trek. The Summerland trailhead starts at about 3,800 feet above sea level, while the Box Canyon trailhead is at about 800 feet—but hikers from either direction must cross 6,700-foot Panhandle Gap. ■

24. Grove of the Patriarchs

RATING	DISTANCE	HIKING TIME	
★ ★ ★ ★ ★	1.25 miles round-trip	45 minutes–1.0 hour	
ELEVATION GAIN	HIGH POINT	DIFFICULTY	♿
Negligible	2,200 feet	♦ ◇ ◇ ◇ ◇	No
TRAIL ACCESSIBLE			
Jan Feb Mar Apr May Jun Jul Aug Sep Oct Nov Dec			

The Hike–Closed until Further Notice

This is a very easy, memorable walk through a splendid old-growth forest on an island in the middle of the beautiful Ohanapecosh River.

But this trail was closed in November 2021 when flooding damaged the suspension bridge, cutting off access to one of the park's signature and most popular trails. Contractors removed the bridge in 2023, with work to replace it unlikely to begin before 2026. Depending on funding (repair work falls within the federal highways budget), the new bridge may see improvements, like widening, and would take about two years to reopen to the public. Until then, you can still access the Grove's parking lot, restrooms, and Eastside (Hike 27) and Silver Falls Loop (Hike 25) trails—two good trails to get your big-tree fix, though you might have to scale back expectations. Trails in the Carbon Valley are replete with grand cedars and firs, though trailheads are accessible only via the five-mile Carbon River Bike-Hike trail, a.k.a. the former Carbon River Road that is now closed to cars. We're keeping this entry in the book in hopes the Grove of the Patriarchs reopens earlier than expected.

Getting There

From the park's Stevens Canyon Entrance on Highway 123, proceed a short distance east, across the Ohanapecosh River bridge, to the trailhead parking area on the right (north) side of the road, elevation 2,200 feet. The lot, which holds about two dozen cars, is often full on summer days. Rangers do not allow parking along the road, but if you can't find a spot, don't give up: Consider parking at the nearby

Roots of a massive western red cedar are protected by a boardwalk

Laughingwater Creek trailhead on Highway 123 or farther south at Ohanapecosh Campground and walking the Eastside Trail upstream, past Silver Falls Loop (Hike 25).

The Trail

Walking this path over the years, we've encountered people of all ages, of all races, from all different countries, and in all shapes and sizes, and all of them exhibit one common behavior: reverence. In

---

PERMITS/CONTACT
Entrance fee; no day-hiking passes required/Ohanapecosh Visitor Center, (360) 569-658l; Longmire Wilderness Information Center, (360) 569-6650

MAPS
Green Trails No. 270, Mount Rainier East; USGS Chinook Pass

TRAIL NOTES
No dogs; kid-friendly—perhaps the best in the park; no bikes

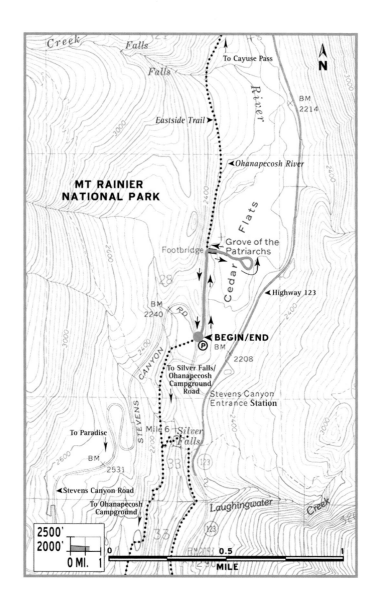

Creek

Falls

Falls

To Cayuse Pass

N

BM
2214

River

Eastside Trail

Ohanapecosh River

MT RAINIER
NATIONAL PARK

Cedar Flats

Grove of the
Patriarchs

Footbridge

Highway 123

BM
2240

RD

BEGIN/END

P

BM

2208

To Silver Falls/
Ohanapecosh
Campground
Road

CANYON

Stevens Canyon
Entrance Station

STEVENS

To Paradise

Mile 6

Silver
Falls

BM
2531

123

Stevens Canyon Road

To Ohanapecosh
Campground

Laughingwater

Creek

Y23

2500'
2000'

0 MI.   1

0   0.5   1
MILE

the Grove of the Patriarchs, you don't run, you don't shout, you don't cavort or gripe. It would be like goofing off in church, which is what this grove of massive western hemlock, western red cedars, and Douglas fir is to multiple generations of Northwest nature lovers. The Grove is one of the more popular destinations in Mount Rainier National Park, and one of the more memorable stands of old-growth anywhere in the country.

The guardian of all this arboreal splendor is the Ohanapecosh River, which forms a protective ring around the small island hosting the Patriarchs, thus keeping them from fire over the centuries. The result is a stirring monument to tenacity: dozens of trees more than 25 feet in circumference—some as much as 50 feet around—and up to one thousand years old.

To get to them, walk the flat, pleasant path upstream from the always-crowded trailhead, beneath several lovely old red cedars, to a crossing of the Ohanapecosh at just less than half a mile. Walk across the steel suspension bridge—the sign says one body at a time, so on a busy day you might have to wait your turn—and follow the trail a short distance to the first really, really big tree, a contorted red cedar, on your left.

Here begins a grand addition to the trail: A raised wooden board-walk, which will carry you on a 0.3-mile loop beneath the Patriarchs. The boardwalk was two years in the making, and is one of the best user-fee-supported projects we've seen in the Northwest. Fortunately, it survived the massive 2006 floods, although the suspension bridge crossing the river to reach it was heavily damaged. The boardwalk pro-tects the old giants' roots and bark from excessive—and damaging—tree hugging and cavorting by visitors. Take your pictures next to the massive Twin Firs, and by all means, take your time walking through here: It's a true treat, in any weather. ■

25. Silver Falls Loop

RATING	DISTANCE	HIKING TIME	
★★★★	3-mile loop	1.5 hours	
ELEVATION GAIN	HIGH POINT	DIFFICULTY	♿
330 feet	2,200 feet	◆ ◇ ◇ ◇ ◇	No
	TRAIL ACCESSIBLE		
	Jan Feb Mar Apr May Jun Jul Aug Sep Oct Nov Dec		

The Hike

Take an easy walk from Ohanapecosh Campground to Silver Falls, one of the park's most impressive lower-altitude sights. Note: If you're looking to see some big trees in the wake of the temporary closure of the Grove of the Patriarchs (Hike 24), this is a good place.

Getting There

Drive to Ohanapecosh Campground, elevation 1,870 feet, located on Highway 123 about 1.8 miles south of the Stevens Canyon Entrance to Mount Rainier National Park. The trail begins at the end of camping loop B, the first to your right at the bottom of the hill as you enter the campground. Drive around the loop and park in one of about a dozen day-use spots, if available. If not, you might have to park back up the hill, at the Ohanapecosh Ranger Station, and walk a half mile back to the trailhead. (Do not, as some guidebooks suggest, park

---

PERMITS/CONTACT

Entrance fee; no day-hiking passes required/Ohanapecosh Visitor Center, (360) 569-6581; Longmire Wilderness Information Center, (360) 569-6650

MAPS

Green Trails No. 270, Mount Rainier East, and No. 302, Packwood; USGS Ohanapecosh Hot Springs and Chinook Pass

TRAIL NOTES

No dogs; kid-friendly; no bikes

The Ohanapecosh River rips through a gorge near Silver Falls

in front of the Ohanapecosh Visitor Center. Those spots have been changed to short-term parking, and you risk being towed.)

The Trail

This trail may well be responsible for what you hold in your hand. The Silver Falls Trail is one of the first Northwest hiking memories still accessible in the cluttered hard drive of this author's brain. He can vaguely

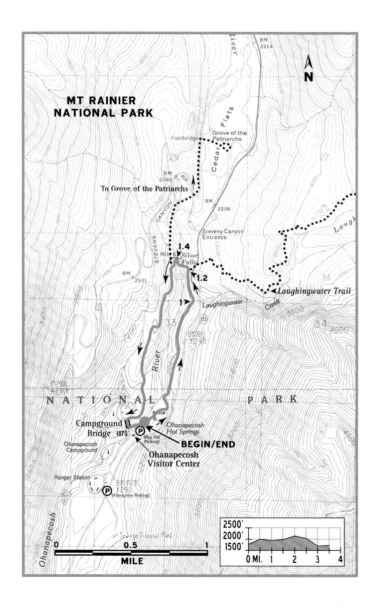

MT RAINIER
NATIONAL PARK

Grove of the
Patriarchs

Footbridge

To Grove of the Patriarchs

BM
2240

BM
2208

Stevens Canyon
Entrance

1.4
Mile 6 *Silver Falls*

BM
2531

1.2

1

Laughingwater

Laughingwater Trail

Creek

N A T I O N A L

P A R K

Campground
Bridge 1870'

(Day-Use
Parking)

Ohanapecosh
Hot Springs

BEGIN/END

Ohanapecosh
Campground

Ohanapecosh
Visitor Center

Ranger Station

BMRB28
X290
(Alternative Parking)

Sewage Disposal Plant

Ohanapecosh

0	0.5	1

MILE

2500'				
2000'				
1500'				
0 MI.	1	2	3	4

remember setting off on the path with his older sister, both fitted with tiny day packs, and returning with the feeling he'd really accomplished something. More than three decades later, not much has changed: You'll still feel like you've accomplished something, no matter your age or ability. It's a popular trail, one of the first to melt out in the spring. Expect plenty of company from the sprawling campground, one of Rainier's prime overnight spots.

This path proceeds at a pleasant grade upstream, following the stunningly crystal-clear Ohanapecosh River (thanks to mostly inactive glaciers at its source, it doesn't carry the glacial flour of most Rainier rivers). At **1.0** mile, cross lovely Laughingwater Creek and reach a junction with the Laughingwater Creek Trail at **1.2** miles. Walk over a short rise to Silver Falls at **1.4** miles, one of the more impressive gushers in the park. Come in the early summer if you want to witness the really big splash. The trail crosses the river as it plunges below the falls into a steep gorge. On the far side, follow the path up to a viewpoint near the top of the falls.

You can return the way you came, but it's not much farther to complete the loop from here. Above the overlook, turn left on the Eastside Trail and stay left again where the Cowlitz Divide Trail branches off. You'll gain altitude steadily for the next three-fourths mile or so, entering a quiet, dark forest and eventually descending back to Ohanapecosh Campground on the west side of the river.

Note: If you're pressed for time and just want to see Silver Falls, you can also reach it via a short, steep hike down the Laughingwater Creek Trail, along Highway 123 north of Ohanapecosh Campground.

Going Farther

From the Eastside Trail junction above Silver Falls, you can continue north on the Eastside Trail for a long half mile, and about 250 vertical feet, along a beautiful stretch of the river to Stevens Canyon Road and the Grove of the Patriarchs Trail (Hike 24, temporarily closed). You can combine both hikes for a satisfying round-trip of about 5.5 miles from Ohanapecosh Campground. ∎

26. Three Lakes

RATING	DISTANCE	HIKING TIME
★★★★☆	12.0 miles round-trip	6.0 hours

ELEVATION GAIN	HIGH POINT	DIFFICULTY	♿
2,520 feet	4,670 feet	♦♦♦♦	No

TRAIL ACCESSIBLE
Jan Feb Mar Apr May Jun **Jul Aug Sep Oct** Nov Dec

The Hike

The strain of this climb to three shallow subalpine lakes is lessened greatly by the solitude and the excellent trail, evenly graded and smooth from beginning to end.

Getting There

From the park's Stevens Canyon Entrance on Highway 123, drive 0.2 mile west on Highway 123 to the wide shoulder parking area on the right side of the road. The trailhead, elevation 2,150 feet, is up the road about 100 feet on the opposite side of the highway.

The Trail

The hike to Three Lakes is long and the rewards in terms of grand views are few, but if you are looking for solitude and the chance of seeing or hearing elk in the fall, this is the trail to take. Perhaps because it lacks vistas of Rainier, or possibly because of its length, the Three Lakes

---

PERMITS/CONTACT
Entrance fee; no day-hiking passes required/Ohanapecosh Visitor Center, (360) 569-6581; Longmire Wilderness Information Center, (360) 569-6650

MAPS
Green Trails No. 271, Bumping Lake; USGS Ohanapecosh Hot Springs

TRAIL NOTES
No dogs; no bikes

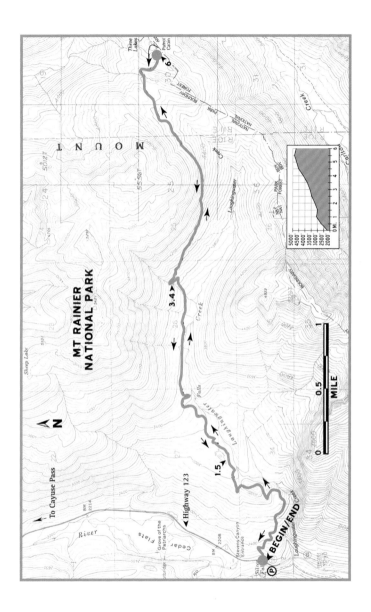

The middle of Three Lakes

Trail sees relatively little use, especially in the autumn. That's too bad, because this is one of the finest trails in the park. The grade is consistent and never too steep, the tread so smooth and free of roots and rocks that you might fall asleep on the way down. It has the feel of one of the old WPA or CCC trails, especially when you can look down to see two or three switchbacks ahead.

Begin by climbing around a forested knoll above Laughingwater Creek, and then drop briefly on one of those switchbacks to pass a swampy lakelet on the left, 1.5 miles from the trailhead. You'll pass the tiny lake and climb again along a wide, rounded ridge beside the creek, switching back several more times past falls and traversing into forested flats beside the creek. In the autumn, Laughingwater is your only water source, and this is the spot to refresh your supply if you have a filter bottle or pump.

The trail leaves the stream and climbs more steeply, switching back up a steep gravelly side hill 3.4 miles from the trailhead.

You'll climb steadily from this point, and in about a mile enter sub-alpine forest. Trees thin and the trail passes along the fringe of a meadow at about **5.2** miles. Just beyond, you'll round a ridge and begin a descent around a wide gully where elk are likely to be seen or heard in the fall.

The trail rounds a second, sharp ridge and drops steeply past the north shore of the first of the Three Lakes. It rounds the lake to the west, and then climbs gently to the Three Lakes Patrol Cabin between the first and second lakes. The third lake lies about 100 yards to the southeast.

Going Farther

Whoa! Those who have the strength to explore after climbing 6 miles will find a fourth lake just west of the first two and—what's this?—a tiny fifth lake about 200 yards east of the third lake. Let's change the name. ■

CHINOOK PASS

27. Eastside Trail

RATING	DISTANCE	HIKING TIME	
★★★ ☆ ☆	7.25 miles one way	3.0–4.0 hours	
ELEVATION LOSS	**HIGH POINT**	**DIFFICULTY**	♿
1,032 feet	3,232 feet	♦ ♦ ◇ ◇ ◇	No
	TRAIL ACCESSIBLE		
	Jan Feb Mar Apr May **Jun Jul Aug Sep Oct Nov** Dec		

The Hike

Take an uncrowded, heavily forested, all-downstream river walk parallel to Highway 123 through one of Mount Rainier National Park's most scenic river valleys. Note: It's also a good chance to see big trees, in place of the temporary closure of Grove of the Patriarchs (Hike 24).

Getting There

The upper trailhead at 3,230 feet is on Highway 123, about 5 miles south of Cayuse Pass and 6 miles north of the park's Stevens Canyon Entrance. Look for the small, unmarked turnout a half mile south of Highway 123's Deer Creek crossing. The lower trailhead at 2,200 feet is the Grove of the Patriarchs parking area, just inside the Stevens Canyon Entrance (Hikes 24 and 25).

PERMITS/CONTACT
Entrance fee; no day-hiking passes required/
Longmire Wilderness Information Center, (360) 569-6650

MAPS
Green Trails No. 270, Mount Rainier East; USGS Chinook Pass

TRAIL NOTES
No dogs; kid-friendly—but they are likely to find it monotonous; no bikes

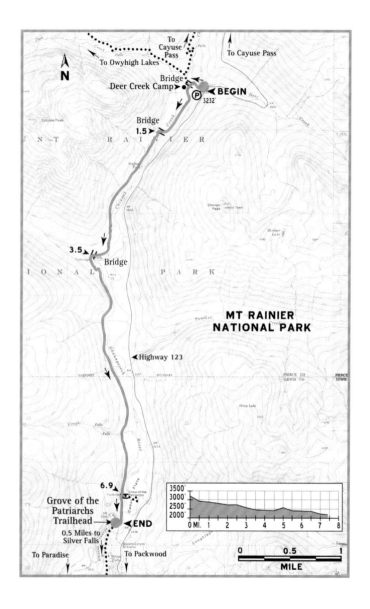

To
Cayuse
Pass

To Cayuse Pass

To Owyhigh Lakes

Bridge

Deer Creek Camp►

Ⓟ ◄BEGIN
3232'

N

Bridge
1.5►

M O U N T   R A I N I E R

Double Peak

3.5►

Bridge

N A T I O N A L   P A R K

Shriner
Peak

Shriner
Lake

MT RAINIER
NATIONAL PARK

◄Highway 123

PIERCE CO
LEWIS CO

PIERCE
LEWIS

Sheep Lake

6.9►

Grove of the
Patriarchs
Trailhead

◄END

0.5 Miles to
Silver Falls

To Paradise

To Packwood

3500'
3000'
2500'
2000'
0 MI. 1   2   3   4   5   6   7   8

0   0.5   1
MILE

Canadian dogwood, a.k.a. bunchberry, grows along the Ohanapecosh River

The Trail

This is one of our favorite walks for early or late season at Rainier and one of the most pleasant river walks in the park—a great choice anytime, but especially when higher-altitude trails are shrouded in fog and that indefatigable, car-wash rain. The Eastside Trail—little used by Rainier standards—is usually hikeable by early June, and remains so until the snow flies and the roads to the trailhead close. It's a consistently cool, pleasant, private walk through heavy forest in the Chinook Creek and Ohanapecosh River drainages. Arrange to be dropped off at the upper trailhead, and it's a painless downhill walk that most people can do in half a day.

From the upper trailhead, drop quickly 0.4 mile to Deer Creek Camp, turn left (south) and have at it. Don't expect to see the river all the way down; it's out of sight for much of the way, but never far off. Don't worry: it's worth waiting for those moments when the trail reconnects you to the water. Several waterfalls are visible along the route, and highlights include beautiful, whitewater-stream crossings on footlogs at **1.5** miles (Chinook Creek) and **3.0** miles (Ohanapecosh River). You'll wish you'd brought your camera.

The route follows the Ohanapecosh drainage the rest of the way down from the latter crossing. At about 6.4 miles south of Deer Creek Camp, you'll rejoin Rainier's teeming tourist masses at the junction with the Grove of the Patriarchs Trail, which is temporary closed due to washouts.

Going Farther

Add 3 *very steep* (hence our suggested start) miles to the north end of the one-way trip by beginning at the large, unmarked parking area along Highway 123 just south of Cayuse Pass. Or begin all the way up at Chinook Pass and add 1.3 miles more. Tack on an additional 2.25 miles to the south end by continuing down the Eastside Trail to the Silver Falls Trail and, ultimately, Ohanapecosh Campground (Hike 25). ■

28. Naches Peak Loop

RATING	DISTANCE	HIKING TIME	
★★★★★	4.5-mile loop	2.0–3.0 hours	
ELEVATION GAIN	HIGH POINT	DIFFICULTY	♿
700 feet	5,900 feet	♦ ◇ ◇ ◇ ◇	No
TRAIL ACCESSIBLE			
Jan Feb Mar Apr May Jun **Jul Aug Sep Oct** Nov Dec			

The Hike

Embark on a glorious, scenic journey atop the Cascade Crest, with great wildflowers, fall colors, and sweeping vistas of the east side of Mount Rainier.

Getting There

From Enumclaw, follow Highway 410 about 50 miles to Chinook Pass, elevation 5,400 feet. Parking for this hike is available at Tipsoo Lake

Picnic Area (requiring a National Park entrance or annual pass), and along the highway between the picnic area and the pass, but it's preferable to proceed east of the pass to the parking lots on either side of the highway. The Pacific Crest Trail (PCT) lot (requiring a Northwest Forest Pass) on the left side is the largest and most convenient. From there, hike the PCT about a quarter mile south to the loop's starting point: the pedestrian highway overpass at the summit.

The Trail

On a clear summer or crisp autumn day, this might be the finest day hike in Washington. Plenty of hands shoot up with competitors, but it's hard to argue this hike's attractions: a smooth, even grade, thanks to tens of thousands of pounding feet and the loving care of trail crews. A very gradual grade, especially if you hike the loop in a clockwise direction. A beautiful alpine valley studded with mirror-like tarns, acres of wildflowers, and, in the fall, wild blueberries and stupendous crimson red bushes. And oh, yeah, there's that big mountain over there, shining in all her glory to the west for about half the hike.

Take our word for it and hike the loop clockwise, which just seems to be the *right* way to do this hike. In the first mile, the Pacific Crest Trail rises gently, traversing a slope above a lush valley, where wildflowers will be peeking up at you from mid-July to mid-August. At about **1.0** mile, you'll note a fine, glassy little tarn to the left. The trail climbs slowly and steadily from here through a rocky alpine bowl,

PERMITS/CONTACT
National Parks Service or USFS Northwest Forest Pass required/Snoqualmie Ranger District, Enumclaw Service Center, (360) 825-6585 or Longmire Wilderness Information Center, (360) 569-6650

MAPS
Green Trails No. 270, Chinook Pass and No. 271, Bumping Lake; USGS Chinook Pass, Cougar Lake, White River Park, and Norse Peak

TRAIL NOTES
Dogs okay—for only half(!) the hike; kid-friendly; no bikes

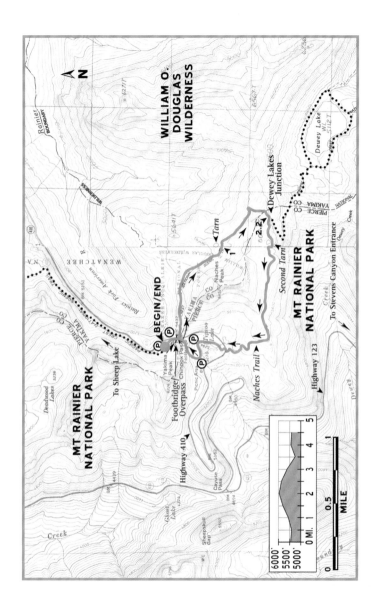

with spacious eastern views, beautiful enough to make you forget you haven't seen Rainier yet. Keep your eyes peeled for elk. Eventually the trail climbs several gentle switchbacks to a ridge top southeast of 6,452-foot Naches Peak. Here, about 2.2 miles in, you'll enter the national park and leave the PCT, which drops down to Dewey Lakes, skips across a bunch more mountains, and eventually dumps you out in Mexico.

Back here closer to home, continue straight on what now is the Naches Trail, which leads you to fine views of Mount Adams and the Goat Rocks, to the south. Before long, Rainier comes into view, framed by a series of splendorous, rolling alpine meadows that are adorned with wildflowers in summer and crimson shrubbery in the fall. Passing another small tarn, you'll begin to drop rapidly back toward the highway. Cross the road at about **4.0** miles and find the nature trail around Tipsoo Lake, which ultimately leads back up through the draw to the overpass and parking area.

Descending toward one of the picturesque tarns on Naches Peak Loop

A word to the wise about dogs: You'll see lots of them on the first portion of this trail, because it's the PCT and, well, dogs are allowed on the PCT, as are horses, llamas, sheep, domesticated wolverines, US senators, and other four-legged creatures. However, at the trail junction 2.2 miles into the hike, you will re-enter the national park, where dogs are expressly forbidden on trails. Your choices at this point are as follows: 1) Go back the way you came and completely miss the best part of the hike; 2) send your dog back on his own, instructing him to open a cold one and fire up the air conditioner in the Blazer; 3) hide the dog in your day pack, beneath the Power Bars; 4) build a fire and cook and eat your dog, thus ensuring you'll have the strength to continue; or 5) wantonly and openly defy the law, risking Lord-knows-what kind of retribution. No pressure or anything, but it's all up to you.

Going Farther

At the park border, you can follow the PCT almost 700 vertical feet down to Dewey Lakes, adding about 2.25 miles to the loop hike (5 miles if you hike all the way around the larger lake). ■

29. Sheep Lake

RATING	DISTANCE	HIKING TIME	
★★★☆☆	3.8 miles round-trip	2.0 hours	
ELEVATION GAIN	HIGH POINT	DIFFICULTY	⚲
330 feet	**5,730 feet**	◆ ◇ ◇ ◇ ◇	**No**
(SHEEP LAKE)	(SHEEP LAKE)	(SHEEP LAKE)	
967 feet	**6,367 feet**	◆ ◆ ◇ ◇ ◇	
(SOURDOUGH GAP)	(SOURDOUGH GAP)	(SOURDOUGH GAP)	

TRAIL ACCESSIBLE											
Jan	Feb	Mar	Apr	May	Jun	**Jul**	**Aug**	**Sep**	**Oct**	Nov	Dec

The Hike

The possibility of sunshine on this family hike east of the Cascade Crest makes the climb to a clear alpine lake more inviting. By climbing steeply another mile on the Pacific Crest Trail, you'll gain a great view of Rainier from 6,367-foot Sourdough Gap.

Getting There

From Enumclaw, follow Highway 410 about 50 miles over Chinook Pass to the second big parking area on the left side of the road, just outside the Mount Rainier National Park boundary. The trailhead, elevation 5,400 feet, is located at the horse loading ramp at the east end of the parking area.

The Trail

A wonderful family hike, Sheep Lake is an underutilized trail that will get you (and your leashed pooch, even) to a splendid alpine lake—the likes of which you usually have to abuse your knees to get to. Not so here, where a gentle path traverses more than a mile along a slope, with expansive views into the leeward Cascades, and beyond into the dry side, before climbing gently through the trees and opening to a magnificent place to have lunch, or even make camp.

Start out walking near the horse-loading area, behind two candidates for the World's Least-Pleasant-Outhouse Award. The walk along the southeastern-facing slope from the trailhead is nearly flat, and in midsummer you'll be able to take in lupine, bear grass, paintbrush and other colorful wildflowers on slopes above and below you. Don't forget to occasionally look back over your right shoulder

PERMITS/CONTACT
USFS Northwest Forest Pass required/Snoqualmie Ranger District, Enumclaw Service Center, (360) 825-6585

MAPS
Green Trails No. 271, Bumping Lake and No. 270, Mount Rainier East; USGS Chinook Pass

TRAIL NOTES
Leashed dogs okay; kid-friendly

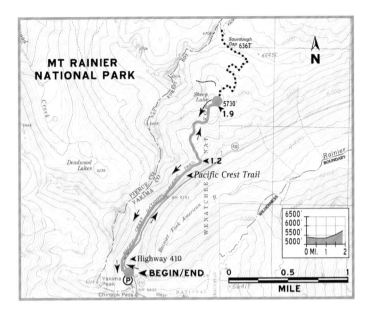

to take in Noble Peak. The only distraction here is Highway 410, snaking along far below you. But with its typically light traffic loads, it's not much of one.

At about 1.2 miles, the trail climbs gradually into the forest and toward a ridgeline. Don't worry: you'll be going through a gap in it, not up and over. The final half mile continues to ascend gently, now in the shade. Get ready: the sensation of walking out of the trees and into the green-shrouded valley holding crystal-clear Sheep Lake makes a magnificent memory. Great lunch spots abound here; it's clearly also a well-used overnight spot for backpackers, and would make an excellent first-time-out overnight trip for children.

This hike is a winner, and the last time we visited on a crystal-clear July day (midweek, granted) we encountered only a small handful of other hikers. It's a great trail to keep in mind on days when the nearby Naches Peak Loop is overcrowded. Note that on hot days, the slopeside first/last section of this trail affords no shade; bring a

Green meadows and crystal clear water await hikers at Sheep Lake

hat and your sunscreen. In the late summer/early fall, it's a great trail for huckleberry picking.

Going Farther

The PCT passes Sheep Lake and becomes a steep, rocky climb for 1 mile and several switchbacks to Sourdough Gap. At 6,376 feet, the gap is 640 feet above the lake. You'll see a way trail just beyond the gap leading to a rocky low saddle to the north. Walk to the saddle on this trail for a good view of Rainier and look down onto Upper Crystal Lake (Hike 31). It is a short but steep climb down to the lake, where you could link with the Crystal Lakes Trail for a one-way or key-exchange hike—assuming you could convince someone to make the longer, steeper climb from the Crystal Lakes trailhead. ■

WHITE RIVER/ SUNRISE

30. Noble Knob

RATING	DISTANCE	HIKING TIME	
★★★★	7.0 miles round-trip	3.5 hours	
ELEVATION GAIN 800 feet	**HIGH POINT** 6,011 feet	**DIFFICULTY** ♦♦♦	👤 No
	TRAIL ACCESSIBLE Jan Feb Mar Apr May Jun Jul Aug Sep Oct Nov Dec		

The Hike

Walk along a sunny ridge blanketed by purple lupine to a splendid view of the east side of Rainier and the icy stretch of Emmons Glacier.

Getting There

Via Corral Pass: From Enumclaw, drive 31.6 miles east on State Route 410 to Corral Pass Road 7174. (If you reach the national park boundary, you have gone too far.) Turn left (east) and proceed 6.7 miles to a trailhead on the left side of the road, just before the large developed parking area. This small parking area at the trailhead proper holds up to six vehicles.

Via Forest Road 72/Dalles Ridge: From Enumclaw, drive 20.3 miles east on State Route 410 to Greenwater Road 70, about a half mile beyond Greenwater. Turn left (north) onto Road 70 and proceed about 5 miles to Road 72 (Twenty-eight Mile Creek Road). Turn right (south) onto Road 72 and follow for 4.1 miles to a small trailhead on the left side of the road.

PERMITS/CONTACT
USFS Northwest Forest Pass required/Snoqualmie Ranger District, Enumclaw Service Center, (360) 825-6585

MAPS
Green Trails No. 239, Lester; USGS Noble Knob

TRAIL NOTES
Leashed dogs okay; kid-friendly, bikes okay

The Trail

Save this hike for a late summer day when you can see forever, because you can definitely see forever along this trail. Okay, maybe "forever" is a slight exaggeration. But with the number of close-up views of Rainier, "forever" will seem irrelevant.

From this former lookout site, gaze west to Rainier and the Emmons Glacier, where you can see with the naked eye climbing routes etched into the ice, and with binoculars, watch climbers negotiating the massive crevasse at the top of the route. If you've already been there and done that, take the hike to Noble Knob on a day when you can't see any of that stuff. Wildflowers are more showy in the diffuse light provided by fog and you won't be troubled by squadrons of horseflies.

There's one challenge of note here: there are multiple ways to access this trail, and the resulting hikes sometimes combine pure path with old roadways. It's a confusing area; signage is sketchy. We've known people who have come here intending to take one route, mistakenly took the other, and never really figured it out until later. The route combining the largest/best developed trailhead with the most pleasant day hike is the route from the Corral Pass Trailhead. But the trail also can be accessed in its upper reaches via a smaller, more obscure trailhead on Dalles Ridge, off Forest Road 72 (Twenty-eight Mile Creek Road). Even though much of the hike's altitude can be gained by car using the upper trailhead(s), we strongly recommend the former approach, with the major caveat that the access road to Corral Pass is consistently steep and rough, usually not suited to low- clearance vehicles, and in fact was closed for some time. If that occurs again, or if the road is gated, use the upper trailhead (both are described in Getting There, opposite page).

If you start from the trailhead near Corral Pass campground, two trails join a short distance to the north. The path that climbs east from here gains and loses several hundred feet and is longer by a half mile, while the northerly trail simply traverses the mountainside. It's best to stay left on the main trail. In the first half mile, it traverses through shady alpine forest before striking the junction with

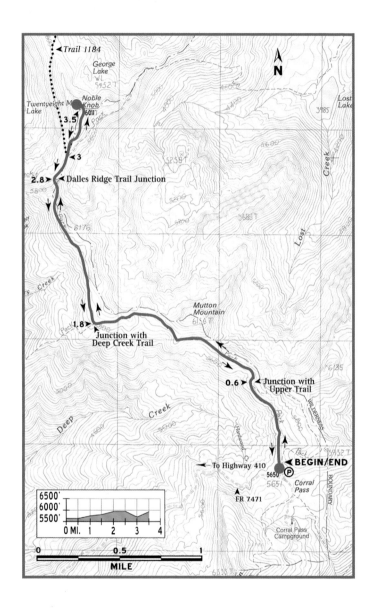

Trail 1184

George Lake
WL
5952 T

Twentyeight Mile Lake

Noble Knob
6011'

3.5

3

2.8 ◄ Dalles Ridge Trail Junction

6176

1.8 ◄ Junction with Deep Creek Trail

Mutton Mountain
6156 T

0.6 ◄ Junction with Upper Trail

Deep Creek

To Highway 410

BEGIN/END
5650'
Corral Pass

FR 7471

Corral Pass Campground

Lost Lake
3985

Lost Creek

5932 T

WILDERNESS BOUNDARY

6135

6880 T

5258 T

6635 T

Elevation					
6500'					
6000'					
5500'					

0 MI. 1 2 3 4

0 .... 0.5 1
MILE

the upper trail at **0.6** mile. Keep left and walk into open hillside created by an old forest fire now overgrown with bear grass, lupine, and other alpine wildflowers.

At **1.8** miles, you'll arrive at the junction with the Deep Creek Trail. Stay right and hike along the ridge, drop to a wide, flat saddle, climb a steep hillside, and round a ridge to traverse open hillside and alpine evergreen groves to a rocky peak directly south of Noble Knob.

The trail rounds the peak and drops steeply to a switchback and junction with the Dalles Ridge Trail at **2.8** miles. Keep right and drop to the flat saddle below Noble Knob, directly to the north.

You'll find a junction with two trails at the flat saddle, **3.0** miles from the trailhead. Stay right at the first fork and, in 10 feet, left at the second fork. The way to Noble Knob briefly climbs the west shoulder before switching back and, in a climbing traverse, circling the peak to the east to arrive at the summit in 0.5 mile. Just below the rocky summit is a wide, flat campsite for picnics with a great mountain view, complete with a 10-foot rock scramble to a nice-looking knob that might even be described as noble.

Going Farther
Lake George, directly below Noble Knob to the north, is the closest of several spots to cool off on a hot day. Follow the trail back to the three-way trail junction and turn right on Trail 1184, which traverses under the west side of Noble Knob. At about 0.6 mile from the trail junction, look for a way trail leading right in 0.2 mile to the lake. ■

31. Crystal Lakes

RATING	DISTANCE	HIKING TIME	
★★★★	6.3 miles round-trip	3.5 hours	
ELEVATION GAIN	HIGH POINT	DIFFICULTY	♿
2,300 feet	5,825 feet	♦♦♦	No
	TRAIL ACCESSIBLE		
	Jan Feb Mar Apr May Jun Jul Aug Sep Oct Nov Dec		

The Hike

This is an increasingly steep trail to two alpine lakes whose clarity may have something to do with their name.

Getting There

From the junction of Highway 410 and Crystal Mountain Boulevard, follow Highway 410 south for 4.6 miles to the trailhead, elevation 3,500 feet, just across the road from the former site of a Washington Department of Transportation equipment shed.

The Trail

The hike to Crystal Lakes is a popular one, especially in the summer. But those who wait until fall will be rewarded with fewer crowds and—promise not to tell anyone—some of the finest huckleberries in the known universe.

It was at Crystal Lakes, back in 1982, that strange, purple, cloven footprints were found on the trail leading down from the upper lake. Because no purple track led up to the lake, it was first believed by some Naches Tavern regulars in nearby Greenwater that aliens had landed at the lakes. Later the tracks were found to be those of a bull elk which had wandered through the huckleberry patch west of the lake and left berry-juice hoofprints for a half mile down the trail. Feel free to check our research on this point.

The trail begins climbing immediately in switchbacks through thick forest. It's only moderately steep at this point and on parts of the pathway you can actually catch your breath before the next hill.

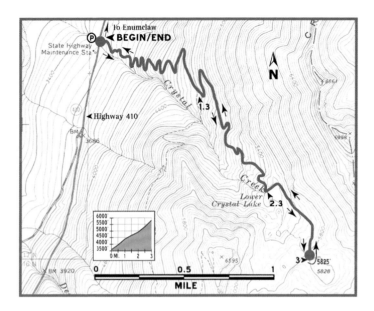

At **1.3** miles, you'll find the Crystal Peak Trail junction. Stay left, here—unless you'd like to climb 1.7 miles to a viewpoint with a stunning view of Rainier. That's something you'll not get at the lakes.

Hikers headed for the lakes begin a steeper climb past the junction, emerging from the forest onto an avalanche slope about 1.5 miles from the trailhead. The route crosses the path of the slide several times as it switches back to the lakes. Near the top of the avalanche

PERMITS/CONTACT
Entrance fee; no day-hiking passes required/
Sunrise Visitor Center, (360) 663-2425

MAPS
Green Trails No. 270, Mount Rainier East; USGS White River

TRAIL NOTES
No dogs; kid-friendly; no bikes

path, you'll get a great view of Mount Rainier and the White River valley to the west. The Mountain ducks behind Crystal Peak at this point.

At **2.3** miles, you'll strike a trail that leads down to the lower and smaller Crystal Lake. This might be the best goal for day hikers with small children—but if they've got any hiking left in those small feet, encourage them to march on to the higher lake. Though there are no more switchbacks, the trail steepens and begins a long, ascending traverse up the western slopes of Crystal Mountain. Hikers may spot mountain goats in the rocks above the trail, and elk frequent this area in the fall.

The climb ends at **3.0** miles as the trail rounds the east side of the lake. To find the huckleberries that remain after the great alien invasion of '82, head for the gentle slopes on the west side of the lake. Those of you who have Polartec-lined innards may enjoy a swim in these icy waters.

Going Farther

Though no maintained trail exists, a way trail leads from the upper lake at Crystal Lakes southeast toward Sourdough Gap and the Pacific Crest Trail (PCT). It's possible to turn the Crystal Lakes Trail into a one-way hike by connecting to the PCT via the ridge above Sheep Lake (Hike 29). You can then hike out to Chinook Pass.

In summer, other hikers often make a one-way trek of the Crystal Lakes hike by either climbing the cat track or road—or by riding the chairlift—to the summit of Crystal Mountain Ski Area. From there they descend to the lakes and out to the highway. ∎

32. Owyhigh Lakes

RATING	DISTANCE	HIKING TIME
★ ★ ★ ★	7.0 miles round-trip	3.5 hours

ELEVATION GAIN	HIGH POINT	DIFFICULTY	♿
1,300 feet	5,100 feet	♦ ♦ ◇ ◇ ◇	No

	TRAIL ACCESSIBLE	
	Jan Feb Mar Apr May Jun **Jul Aug Sep Oct** Nov Dec	

The Hike

Enjoy a moderate climb to quiet alpine meadows dotted by shallow lakes that reflect the crags of the Cowlitz Chimneys and Governors Ridge. Hikers with two cars have an 8.8-mile, one-way option.

Getting There

From the park's White River Entrance on Highway 410, drive 2.1 miles to the parking lot on the right side of the road. The trailhead, elevation 3,750 feet, is across the road.

The Trail

The hike to Owyhigh Lakes is not recommended for neurotics, simply because you'll go nuts trying to figure out the best time for this walk. If you go in the summer, you'll have the opportunity to wade through mounds of wildflowers. If you go in the fall, you'll miss most of the wildflowers, but have a far greater opportunity of sharing the lake view with herds of elk. Perhaps the best advice is this:

PERMITS/CONTACT
Entrance fee; no day-hiking passes required/
Sunrise Visitor Center, (360) 663-2425

MAPS
Green Trails No. 270, Mount Rainier East; USGS Mount Rainier East

TRAIL NOTES
Kid-friendly

A hint of the open meadows ahead lures hikers on the Owyhigh Lakes trail

if you have trouble deciding, save your neuroses for more important matters. Do the hike once in summer and once in the fall. Maybe because this hike offers no views of that big mound of whipped cream that draws most people to Rainier, this trail usually sees fewer crowds. On an autumn weekday, there's a chance you'll have the lakes all to yourselves.

Begin by walking a short 0.1 mile through forest before starting a series of long switchbacks up the broad shoulder of Tamanos Mountain. The trail is wide and it may seem less steep because of its even grade and smooth tread.

You'll strike the first of six switchbacks at about **0.3** mile, with a view down to the polished boulders of Shaw Creek. The trail continues to climb through deep forest up the ridge, which affords hikers peekaboo views of the road climbing to Sunrise across the White River valley.

The climb through the woods is steady, though never steep enough to discourage young hikers. At **3.0** miles, you'll cross a footlog at Tamanos Creek, where a green meadow marked by a way trail stretches steeply up. Cross the footlog back into forest to a junction with the side trail leading down to Tamanos Creek Camp. Stay to the

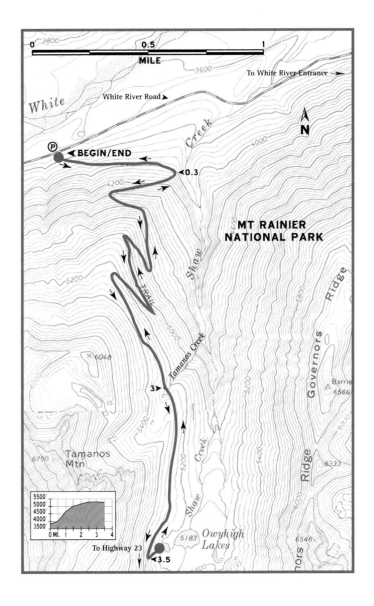

0   3800

0.5

1

MILE

3600

To White River Entrance ➤

White

White River Road ➤

Creek

3800

4000

Ⓟ ◀ **BEGIN/END**

◀ 0.3

4200

4000

4200

MT RAINIER
NATIONAL PARK

5200

Shaw

E TRAIL

5200

5000

5000

5800

Governors Ridge

Barrier
6366

× 6048

Tamanos Creek

5200

3 ➤

5400

6333

Tamanos
Mtn

6790

5200

Shaw Creek

5400

5200

5500'
5000'
4500'
4000'
3500'
0 Mi. 1 2 3 4

6548×

6548×

To Highway 23

5183

Owyhigh
Lakes

◀ 3.5

6333

6790

The payoff: beautiful meadows surrounding the small Owyhigh Lakes

right here, and follow the trail as it levels off and contours the final 0.5 mile into alpine meadowland above Owyhigh Lakes.

The lakes are about 100 feet below the trail on the left, and those visiting the shoreline and meadows around the lakes often leave the trail at first sight of the lakes. No sign marks the lakes and no maintained trail drops into the broad plain around them; hikers who stay on the main trail to the south end of the tarns will find a way trail leading along the inlet stream down to water's edge.

Now, neurotics who have ignored our advice and chosen to go on this hike in the summer can slap and scratch at their many, many mosquito and blackfly bites. Maybe next time, you'll wait until the fall.

Going Farther

Hikers with autos parked at the Owyhigh Lakes trailhead and at the Deer Creek trailhead off Highway 123 (Hike 27) can make a one-way hike by meeting at the 5,400-foot pass about 0.5 mile south of the lakes. This is the high point of the hike and a good place to exchange car keys. From there, one-way hikers would continue 3 miles through alpine meadows and forest, switching back down and descending another 2 miles to Boundary and Deer Creek, and then climbing in steep switchbacks 0.4 mile and 300 feet to the Deer Creek trailhead. ■

33. Summerland

RATING	DISTANCE	HIKING TIME	
★★★★★	8.5 miles round-trip	5.0 hours	
ELEVATION GAIN	HIGH POINT	DIFFICULTY	♿
2,140 feet	5,950 feet	♦♦	No
	TRAIL ACCESSIBLE		
	Jan Feb Mar Apr May Jun Jul Aug Sep Oct Nov Dec		

The Hike

A memorable—and often very crowded—stroll takes you through several miles of forest lands along Fryingpan Creek, and then steeply up for a final mile to picturesque Summerland Camp, one of the park's most famous subalpine destinations.

Getting There

From the park's White River Entrance on Highway 410, proceed just under 3 miles to the Wonderland Trail's Fryingpan Creek trailhead, elevation 3,810 feet. Parking is on either side of the road; the trail begins on the left (southwest) side, near the bridge. Parking is at a premium here on summer weekends, and rangers frown on parking along the shoulderless highway—groups should consider parking at White River Campground and carpooling to the trailhead.

The Trail

We'll lay out the only drawback right up front: crowds. Don't expect any subalpine solitude here. Summerland, one of the park's most popular day-hike destinations, draws hundreds of hikers on summer weekends. But you'll see why. The walk, almost all on the famed Wonderland Trail, begins gently in cool forest along Fryingpan Creek, with a few sneak peeks of jagged peaks on the far side, but mostly you're surrounded by emerald forest. At about **1.5** miles, the grade steepens a bit. Keep cruising up to about **2.0** miles, where you'll cross a clearing filled with asters and other wildflowers, in season.

At about **3.0** miles, the trail opens up to its one major stream crossing, on footlogs, over Fryingpan Creek. It's a great rest spot; some hikers turn around here, content with the forest walk. If you're going on, break out that do-rag and dunk it in the icy creek: The trail gets steep from here on out, gaining about 800 feet, most of that in the last mile. You'll climb steadily through the trees to a southward bend in the trail, then continue up brushy, steep switchbacks dotted by avalanche lilies in July and August. This portion of the trail can stay snow covered until late July; use caution.

At **4.2** miles, the trail levels out in flat-out gorgeous meadows and subalpine forest near Summerland, a backcountry camp where the five designated sites are tucked into a grove of trees near the stone shelter. All are usually booked solid throughout the summer. Well, duh— aside from the outhouse, everything here looks grand: abundant

PERMITS/CONTACT
Entrance fee; no day-hiking passes required/
Sunrise Visitor Center, (360) 663-2425

MAPS
Green Trails No. 270, Mount Rainier East; USGS White River Park, Chinook Pass, Mount Rainier East, Sunrise

TRAIL NOTES
No dogs; kid-friendly—great way to wear out those 10 and up; no bikes

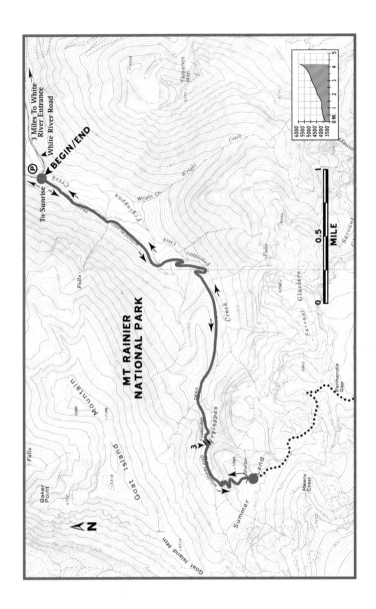

3 Miles To White
River Entrance
White River Road

BEGIN/END

To Sunrise

MT RAINIER
NATIONAL PARK

Goat Island
Mountain

Baker
Point
Falls

Goat Island Mtn

Wright Creek

Fryingpan Creek

Fryingpan Creek

Falls

Creek

Fryingpan Falls

SUMMERLAND

3

Shelter

Summerland

Sarvant Glaciers

Panhandle Gap

Meany Crest

N

0   0.5   1
MILE

6000'
5500'
5000'
4500'
4000'
3500'
0 MI 1 2 3 4 5

wildflowers and wild animals, and postcard views of Rainier, the Fryingpan Glacier, Little Tahoma, and Goat Island Mountain. Take a load off your feet, soak up some sun, and memorize the moment. On a favorable summer day, it doesn't get much better. The trip out is quick and pleasant, assuming you're not fighting a big blister and/or nasty packs of blackflies.

Going Farther

The trail continues another 2 miles and about 850 vertical feet up the rocky moraine of the Fryingpan Glacier to Panhandle Gap, elevation 6,800 feet—worth the trip if you have the time. For a spectacular, one-way shuttle hike, descend south from Panhandle Gap on the Wonderland Trail to Indian Bar Camp. Continue down Cowlitz Divide to Box Canyon (16.6 total miles; Hike 23) or southeast via the Olallie Creek Trail to the Stevens Canyon Entrance or Highway 123 near Ohanapecosh Campground (about 18 total miles). ∎

34. Emmons Moraine/Glacier Basin

RATING	DISTANCE	HIKING TIME
★★★★	4.0 miles round-trip to end of Emmons/6.2 miles round-trip to Glacier Basin	2.0 hours/ 4.0 hours

ELEVATION GAIN	HIGH POINT	DIFFICULTY	♿
850 feet/ 1,650 feet	5,200 feet/ 6,000 feet	♦ ◆ ◆ ◆ ◆ ♦ ♦ ◆ ◆ ◆	No

TRAIL ACCESSIBLE
Jan Feb Mar Apr May Jun **Jul Aug Sep Oct** Nov Dec

The Hike

Hike a river valley to dueling payoffs: a high vista over the massive Emmons Glacier and a great alpine basin in a park area once home to mining activity.

Emmons Glacier and the White River, viewed from high above near Sunrise

Getting There

From the park's White River Entrance on Highway 410, proceed just under 4 miles to the White River Campground turnoff. Turn left and continue 1.5 miles, through the campground, to the hiker and climber day-use parking area on the left (north) side of the road. Walk east on the campground road through Loop D to the Glacier Basin trailhead, elevation 4,350 feet.

The Trail

This isn't just a great hike; it's a great *combination* of hikes, allowing you to design a daylong outing to suit the time available or just your mood. And we're happy to report that though much of the lower portions of this trail were washed out by devastating flooding in 2006, hard work by trail crews in the succeeding decade has rendered most of that just a fading bad-weather memory. The trail's new course is a more pleasant, less rocky walk than it was before the deluge. Although small slides sometimes plague the first quarter-mile of the walk, the trail is now one of the very best places to get up close and personal with what unfortunately is becoming, in this era of vanishing ice, a rare sight—a truly massive glacier. (That's especially true now that the Carbon Glacier Trail, on the other side of the mountain, has

PERMITS/CONTACT
Entrance fee; no day-hiking passes required/
Sunrise Visitor Center, (360) 663-2425

MAPS
Green Trails No. 270, Mount Rainier East; USGS Sunrise

TRAIL NOTES
No dogs; kid-friendly; no bikes

become a much longer hike due to the closure of the Carbon Glacier Road.) From White River Campground, the path ascends gently on and off of an old road grade along the Inter Fork of the White River. Believe it or not, mining equipment made its way through here from the 1890s through the 1950s, thankfully with little success.

About 1.0 mile up the way, the Emmons Moraine Trail crosses the creek and exits to the left (south). Hike up the loose sand on the moraine as far as you like. After about only about a quarter mile up the trail, you can climb atop the moraine for a killer view of the ground-out path of the massive Emmons Glacier—the largest by volume in the Lower 48 states—and on up the valley to the foot of the glacier itself. Look closely: This icy behemoth, although a shadow of its former self, is actually bigger than it looks. Rocky debris from a gigantic rockslide off Little Tahoma Peak covered the middle of the glacier decades ago; the slide is only now making its way down toward the glacier's toe. The maintained trail ends in half a mile at 5,200 feet, but there's no need to go all the way to the end for the view.

To reach Glacier Basin, return to the main trail and keep ascending gradually until about 2.5 miles, where there is some old mining junk along the trail. From here, the grade steepens for the rest of the way to Glacier Basin Camp at **3.1** miles, where wildflowers burst forth in season. Most of Rainier is blocked from view, but there's plenty to see. Watch for mountain goats on the slopes of Mount Ruth and The Wedge, at the head of the basin.

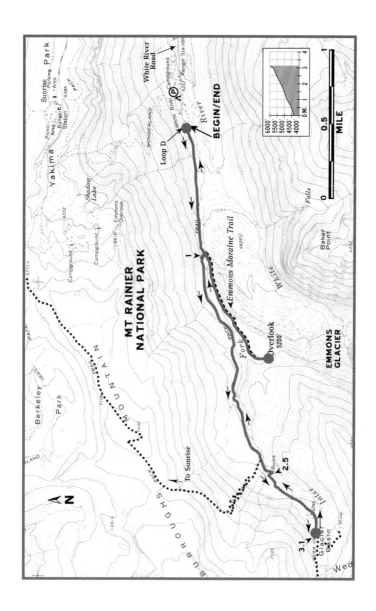

Going Farther

A number of way trails sprout out from the basin, including a steep path down to the Inter Fork and a climbers' trail up to 9,400-foot Camp Schurman, tucked behind Steamboat Prow at the junction of the Winthrop and Emmons Glaciers. Schurman is the departure point for Rainier summit expeditions up the Emmons Glacier. At this writing, many of those hikes were guided commercially by International Mountain Guides, the company owned by noted Himalayan mountaineer Eric Simonson, of Mallory and Irvine Research Expedition fame.

You can also reach Glacier Basin on an all-downhill, one-way route by beginning at Sunrise. Hike the Sunrise Rim and Burroughs Loop Trails (Hike 37) east to the Burroughs Mountain Trail, plunge downhill on steep switchbacks to Glacier Basin (6.3 miles), and exit east at White River Campground (9.5 miles). ■

35. Palisades Lakes

RATING	DISTANCE	HIKING TIME
★ ★ ★	7.5 miles round-trip	3.0–4.0 hours
ELEVATION GAIN	**HIGH POINT**	**DIFFICULTY** ♿
1,600 feet	6,150 feet	♦ ♦ ♦ No
	TRAIL ACCESSIBLE	
	Jan Feb Mar Apr May Jun Jul Aug Sep Oct Nov Dec	

The Hike

Descend sharply to find a string of a half-dozen scenic alpine lakes in this protected valley. The Palisades Lakes Trail is a good foul-weather alternative to more exposed hikes at Sunrise, though the lakes can be *very* buggy in midsummer.

Getting There

From the park's White River Entrance on Highway 410, proceed about 11 miles on White River Road to the well-marked Sunrise Point parking area, on a hairpin curve at 6,150 feet. The trail begins across the road, near the crux of the hairpin curve.

The Trail

The Palisades Lakes Trail is an oddity because it starts high and drops like a rock, plummeting more than 500 feet in the first mile. After a series of switchbacks, you'll enter a valley dotted by a half-dozen fine alpine lakes. The first, Sunrise Lake, is dead ahead at the bottom of the hill. But nicer ones await: Take the main path to the right and enter a pleasant, fairly flat stretch of alternating meadows and forest. Clover Lake, the largest in this cluster and a true beauty, complete with a sandy beach, comes up on your right in about **1.5** miles. It's a great picnic spot. And check out the five-way echo that results if you let out a war whoop from the small knoll along the shoreline.

The trail from here climbs a ridgeline, and then drops steeply over the other side to more meadows and a junction, at **2.5** miles. A short spur trail leads up to Hidden Lake, a gorgeous, glacial-cirque lake below Sourdough Mountain. On the opposite side of the main trail, look for Dick Lake Camp and another spur leading to Tom, Dick, and Harry Lakes.

Continue a mostly flat mile north on the main trail, through some great open meadows, to a trail junction. The left fork leads to Upper Palisades Lake and its backcountry campsites. Continue right to see Lower Palisades Lake from near the end of the maintained trail.

Upper Palisades Lake, elevation 5,840 feet, is definite postcard material. It's set below the Palisades, a fascinating formation of striated rock.

PERMITS/CONTACT
Entrance fee; no day-hiking passes required/
Sunrise Visitor Center, (360) 663-2425

MAPS
Green Trails No. 270, Mount Rainier East; USGS Sunrise and White River Park

TRAIL NOTES
No dogs; no bikes

A meadow near Clover Lake, largest of the Palisades Lakes

Wildflowers are glorious here in season. Watch for elk and deer throughout this valley, and remember: Save some gas for the trip out, where you'll climb 900 feet in elevation on the way back to the trail-head. Be prepared for a short but very steep climb up the ridge back to Clover Lake, followed by that blasted last half mile of pure vertical back to the car! Something about saving it for the end makes it twice as ominous. ■

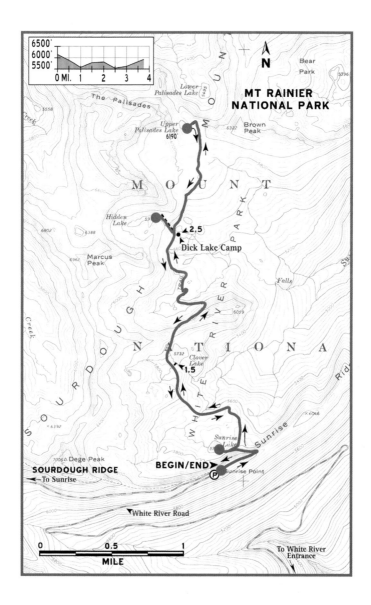

6500'
6000'
5500'
0 MI. 1 2 3 4

N

Bear
Park
5596

Lower
Palisades Lake
5495

**MT RAINIER
NATIONAL PARK**

The Palisades

5558

Creek

Upper
Palisades Lake
6190'

6392

Brown
Peak

M O U N T

Hidden
Lake

59

6802

5388

2.5

Dick Lake Camp

Marcus
Peak

6962

P A R K

Falls

Creek

5732

Clovey
Lake

1.5

N A T I O N A

6099

S O U R D O U G H   M O U N T A I N

6746

6392

5600

Ridg

Sunrise

Sunrise
Lake

BEGIN/END

Dege Peak
7006

SOURDOUGH RIDGE
To Sunrise

Sunrise Point

P

White River Road

6000

0   0.5   1
MILE

To White River
Entrance

36. Silver Forest/Emmons Vista

RATING	DISTANCE	HIKING TIME
★★★☆☆	**2.0 miles round-trip**	**45 minutes**
ELEVATION GAIN	**HIGH POINT**	**DIFFICULTY** ♿
170 feet	**6,400 feet**	◆◇◇◇◇ **No**

TRAIL ACCESSIBLE
~~Jan Feb Mar Apr May Jun~~ **Jul Aug Sep Oct** ~~Nov Dec~~

The Hike

This easy, mostly level stroll leaves the Sunrise complex, ambles to a grand vista of the Emmons Glacier and Mount Rainier, and continues beyond through a pleasant forest of silver firs with more great mountain views.

Getting There

From the park's White River Entrance on Highway 410, proceed 14 miles to Sunrise, elevation 6,400 feet. The trail begins on the south border of the parking area straight across from the Sunrise Ranger Station; follow signs to Emmons Vista.

The Trail

If you're a hiker who wants the best views with the least amount of sweat and blisters, this one's for you. The Silver Forest Trail is an easy walk, slightly downhill at first, about 0.3 mile to Emmons

PERMITS/CONTACT
Entrance fee; no day-hiking passes required/
Sunrise Visitor Center, (360) 663-2425

MAPS
Green Trails No. 270, Mount Rainier East; USGS Sunrise and White River Park

TRAIL NOTES
No dogs; no bikes; easiest Sunrise view hike for kids and seniors

A classic Rainier sight: Emmons Vista on a clear day

Vista, an impressive stone viewing platform with a billion-dollar view of Rainier. Interpretive signs describe the forces behind (and under and all around) the massive Emmons Glacier. On a clear day in midsummer, you can see the ant trail of climbers ascending to the 14,411-foot summit.

Don't stop here, though. The Silver Forest Trail continues east, following the ridgeline, through meadows which, in midsummer, are ablaze with an impressionist painter's palette of orange and magenta paintbrush, blue alpine lupine, lavender alpine asters, yellow daisies, and other magnificent wildflowers. In fall, low huckleberry bushes turn crimson. Rainier is omnipresent to the south. Take your time, breathe in that sweet, thin alpine air, watch for butterflies, and be sure to carry plenty of film. Most of this trail's (small) elevation gain is on the way out.

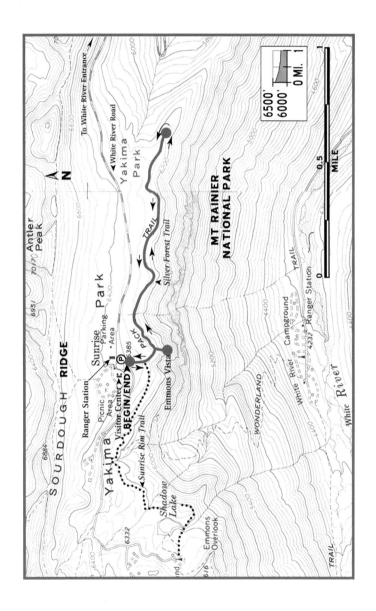

Note: If you're looking for the best pictures of Rainier from here, skip that extra latte and get here in the morning; the sun is directly over The Mountain by midafternoon in summer. Also note that no water is available along the trail.

Going Farther

This hike can be combined with the Sunrise Rim Loop (Hike 37) for a hike of about 5 miles. ■

37. Sunrise Rim Loop

RATING	DISTANCE	HIKING TIME
★★★★	3-mile loop	1.5 hours
ELEVATION GAIN	HIGH POINT	DIFFICULTY ♿
250 feet	6,400 feet	◆ ○ ○ ○ ○ No
	TRAIL ACCESSIBLE	
	Jul Aug Sep Oct	

The Hike

Follow an easy, family-friendly loop that showcases gorgeous wild-flower meadows, mountain views, and plentiful wildlife—all within 1.5 miles of Sunrise Visitor Center.

Getting There

From the park's White River Entrance on Highway 410, proceed 14 miles to Sunrise, elevation 6,400 feet. The trail begins on the south border of the parking area across from the Sunrise Ranger Station; follow signs to Sunrise Camp.

The Trail

Here's your Whitman's Sampler of the Sunrise area: a lightly used route (by Sunrise standards, at least) combining a trail to Sunrise Camp and a park service access road with fine alpine views of its own. From the parking lot, begin at the same south-side trailhead used to access

PERMITS/CONTACT
Entrance fee; no day-hiking passes required/
Sunrise Visitor Center, (360) 663-2425

MAPS
Green Trails No. 270, Mount Rainier East; USGS Sunrise

TRAIL NOTES
No dogs; no bikes; great family hike

the Silver Forest Trail (Hike 36). At the first junction, stay right on the Sunrise Rim Trail. For the next mile, you'll drop gently through open meadows dotted by the stately subalpine firs common in this area, all the while enjoying stupendous views of Rainier and the green forests and meadows of Yakima Park.

At about **0.5** mile, you'll meet a junction with the Wonderland Trail, which drops sharply 2.6 miles to White River Campground. Stay straight on what now is technically the Wonderland Trail, toward Sunrise Camp.

At about **1.0** mile, you'll pass glassy, shallow—and yes, shadowy—Shadow Lake. About a half mile farther is Sunrise Camp, elevation 6,260 feet. In days of yore, this was a car camp, now it's a backcountry site available by reservation (file it away as a good first-time backpacking destination for kids).

For your return, follow the same route you came, or try something new: Walk the (closed) gravel service road departing north from the campground. It's lightly traveled, pleasantly graded, and views are wide open from either side. Keep your eyes peeled for Rocky Mountain elk around the road's first bend. It's an easy walk from here back to Sunrise, although most of the hike's modest elevation gain comes on the way out.

Note: Carry plenty of water—it's scarce along the route.

Going Farther

From the rear of Sunrise Camp, a trail climbs sharply to the top of Burroughs Mountain (Hike 41). You can walk the first 0.25 mile or so to an impressive overlook of the Emmons Glacier.

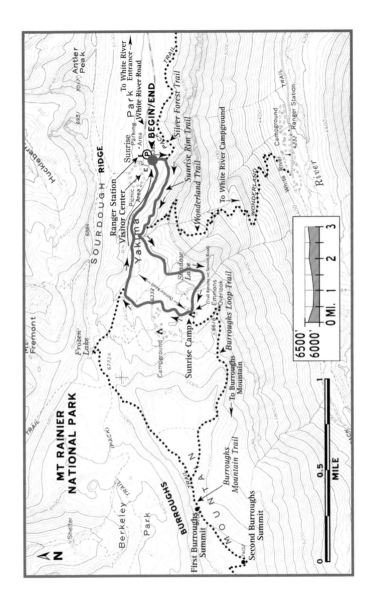

The stunning alpine scenery of Yakima Park

If the weather looks good and your knees feel better, continue on the Burroughs Loop Trail and then the Burroughs Mountain Trail 1.3 miles—and nearly 1,000 vertical feet—up to the First Burroughs summit at 7,300 feet. Note that this may involve a hazardous snowfield crossing before late summer. Follow the Burroughs Loop Trail northeast back to a junction with the Sourdough Ridge Trail at Frozen Lake, and turn right to return to Sunrise. It makes a spectacular loop of about 5.2 miles.

Or, back near Sunrise Camp, follow the Wonderland Trail up to Frozen Lake and walk back to Sunrise via the Sourdough Ridge Trail, making a loop of about 4 miles. ■

38. Sourdough Ridge/Dege Peak

RATING	DISTANCE	HIKING TIME
★ ★ ★	4.0 miles round-trip	1.5 hours

ELEVATION GAIN	HIGH POINT	DIFFICULTY	♿
600 feet	7,006 feet	♦	No

TRAIL ACCESSIBLE
Jan Feb Mar Apr May Jun Jul Aug Sep Oct Nov Dec

The Hike

Take the whole family on this hike and enjoy sweeping views south to Little Tahoma, the Emmons Glacier, and the northeast face of Mount Rainier, and north along the Cascade chain as far as Mount Baker. Be sure to carry plenty of water and sunscreen up—the entire route is exposed to sun.

Getting There

From the park's White River Entrance on Highway 410, proceed 14 miles to Sunrise, elevation 6,400 feet. Begin to the right of the restrooms and walk to the trail's start at the picnic area. On the early portion of the route, follow signs to Dege Peak.

The Trail

On a sunny summer day, the only better place to see the Cascades stretching from Rainier to the north may well be from the summit of The Mountain itself. The Sourdough Ridge Trail, which technically

PERMITS/CONTACT
Entrance fee; no day-hiking passes required/
Sunrise Visitor Center, (360) 663-2425

MAPS
Green Trails No. 270, Mount Rainier East; USGS Sunrise and White River Park

TRAIL NOTES
No dogs; kid-friendly; no bikes

Rainier's summit looms above most day-hiking trails at Sunrise

runs east–west above Sunrise all the way from Sunrise Point to Frozen Lake (Hikes 39 and 40), is a major thoroughfare in the Sunrise area, carrying thousands of hikers to higher-level trailheads, mostly northwest of Sunrise. But the crowds are thinner, and views even grander, if you ascend the broad, graveled entry path from Sunrise and turn right (east) on the Sourdough Ridge Trail and follow the ridgeline toward Dege Peak.

Remember: The ridge top is 6,800 feet, so if you're unaccustomed to exercise at high altitude, you'll be feeling the big squeeze on your lungs. But this is a pleasant, mostly flat walk once the ridge is gained at **0.3** mile. The views are spectacular in both directions, and wildflowers will be magnificent on the south-facing slopes in midsummer.

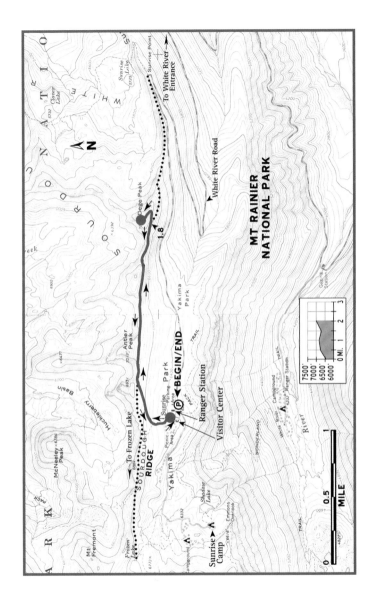

At **1.8** miles, a short spur leads up to the top of Dege Peak, elevation 7,006. It's a supreme vista. Look for Rainier, of course, but also the Sarvent Glaciers below the Cowlitz Chimneys, due south; the White River drainage and Highway 410, to the east; Sunrise and Clover Lakes of the Palisades chain (see Hike 35) directly below to the northeast; and the Stuart Range, Glacier Peak, and Mount Baker far off to the north. If it's very clear, you can even see the Olympic Mountains from here.

Going Farther

If you can arrange for a ride, keep descending down the ridge for another steep mile to the Sunrise Point parking lot, for a one-way hike of about 3 miles. ■

39. Huckleberry Creek/Forest Lake

RATING	DISTANCE	HIKING TIME
★★ ☆☆☆	5.0 miles round-trip	2.5 hours
ELEVATION GAIN	**HIGH POINT**	**DIFFICULTY** ♿
500 feet in, 1,300 feet out	6,900 feet	♦ ♦ ◇◇◇ No

TRAIL ACCESSIBLE
Jan Feb Mar Apr May Jun **Jul Aug Sep Oct** Nov Dec

The Hike

Climb up and over Sourdough Ridge to a pleasant mountain lake. You'll get fewer great Rainier views—but also fewer people—than on other Sunrise-area trails.

Getting There

From the park's White River Entrance on Highway 410, drive 14 miles to Sunrise, elevation 6,400 feet. Begin to the right of the restrooms and walk to the trail's start at the picnic area. Follow signs to the left (west) toward Frozen Lake, and then Huckleberry Creek Trail.

Descending Sourdough Ridge near the Huckleberry Creek Trail junction

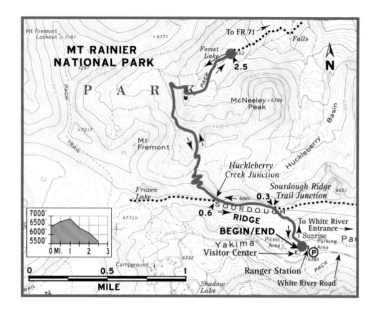

The Trail

The first portion of this hike follows the same route as many other trails in this section: up to the top of Sourdough Ridge, and then a short distance west to a junction with the Huckleberry Creek Trail at **0.6** mile. Follow the Huckleberry Creek Trail right and moments later you'll begin dropping steadily, almost 1,300 feet in a shy 2.0 miles, through a fascinating variety of terrain. The upper portion is rocky and inhospitable (beware of snow lingering here into August most years); the central portion wanders through scenic, subalpine parkland dotted with red heather; the lower area, near Forest Lake, is deciduous forest.

The central portion between 7,317-foot Mount Fremont (left/west) and 6,786-foot McNeeley Peak (right/east), is the most scenic. Keep your eyes peeled for mountain goats on the back side of Fremont.

In season, meadows around Forest Lake (your destination, 2.5 miles) are ripe with wildflowers. Have a hearty lunch and head back up the trail. The view of Rainier as you come over the rise of Sourdough Ridge is unforgettable.

Going Farther

The Huckleberry Creek Trail leads a total of 8.3 miles from Sourdough Ridge to a low trailhead (3,000 feet) on Forest Road 73, in Mount Baker–Snoqualmie National Forest. It's a popular one-way, downhill day hike or backpack route (Forest Lake has one backcountry campsite). ■

40. Frozen Lake/Mount Fremont Lookout

RATING	DISTANCE	HIKING TIME	
★ ★ ★ ★	5.4 miles round-trip	3.0 hours	
ELEVATION GAIN	HIGH POINT	DIFFICULTY	♿
781 feet	7,181 feet	♦ ♦	No
	TRAIL ACCESSIBLE		
	Jul Aug Sep Oct		

The Hike

Enjoy a memorable walk along Sourdough Ridge to a five-way trail junction near Frozen Lake, and beyond to a mountain lookout tower where mountain goats and other wildlife often linger.

Getting There

From the park's White River Entrance, proceed 14 miles to Sunrise, elevation 6,400 feet. Begin to the right of the restrooms and walk to the trail's start at the picnic area. Follow signs to the left (west) toward Frozen Lake.

The Trail

There's really no place like this in the Cascades, the West, the country, or maybe the world. The walk to Frozen Lake and Mount Fremont

PERMITS/CONTACT
Entrance fee; no day-hiking passes required/
Sunrise Visitor Center, (360) 663-2425

MAPS
Green Trails No. 270, Mount Rainier East; USGS Sunrise

TRAIL NOTES
No dogs; kid-friendly—for the older ones; no bikes

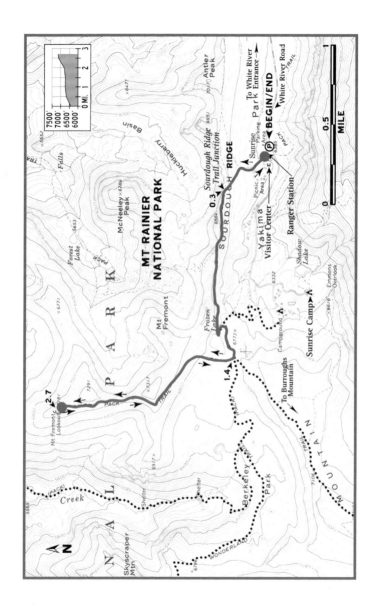

The long, steady rise to Mount Fremont Lookout

is a rite of passage for Northwestern tykes. Many people's first shaky steps off the pavement and onto the moon-rock dust of Rainier's stunning alpine tundra happen along this route. And the fact that it's just the first step to many great leaps gives this hike a special appeal.

The first part of this walk follows the path taken to many other popular hikes in this area: up to Sourdough Ridge, then left (west) on the Sourdough Ridge Trail, with grand views of Rainier to the south and the entire Cascade chain to the north. At one point, you'll stand in a draw on a ridge top no wider than a street, and have trouble deciding which way to focus your attention.

The path drops slightly, crossing a rocky slope (nice trail work, that retaining wall!), and then climbs gently to a hard left-hand turn at Frozen Lake. The lake, a pretty, deep-aqua pool, is fenced off, because it's the drinking water supply for Sunrise. Take the left turn and follow the path around and up to a major trail junction at **1.4** miles. Major as in, sort of mind boggling. No fewer than five trails converge at this point; it's the Rainier alpine hiker freeway interchange. Plop yourself down on a rock here and drink in the views of Rainier (lower flanks), Burroughs Mountain, Yakima Park and Sunrise, and Mount Fremont. You can also take in the vast plains of the Wonderland Trail leading toward Berkeley Park.

You can make this your turnaround point without feeling completely cheated, but far greater splendors await. Follow signs to the Mount Fremont Trail, which skirts Frozen Lake to the north, climbing steadily up the ridge in a long, 1.3-mile straight line with no switchbacks. Don't forget to check your rearview mirror for Rainier—preferably not while you're along the steep drop-off near the top of the trail, on the shoulder of Mount Fremont. The path descends slightly to the lookout at **2.7** miles and 7,181 feet. The view is stunning, from Rainier all the way to the North Cascades. (Be glad you weren't here in the winter of 2006 when a violent storm blew the roof completely off the lookout!) Watch for mountain goats grazing on the slopes nearby, and whatever you do, don't contribute to the further Power Bar addiction of local marmots.

Note: Carry plenty of water—it's scarce along the route.

Going Farther

Burroughs Mountain (Hike 41), Berkeley Park (Hike 42), Sunrise Camp (via the Wonderland Trail), and other destinations all are accessible from the trail super-junction at Frozen Lake. ■

41. Burroughs Mountain

RATING	DISTANCE	HIKING TIME
★★★★★	6.2 miles round-trip via Frozen Lake/ 6.7-mile loop via Sunrise Camp	3.0–4.0 hours

ELEVATION GAIN	HIGH POINT	DIFFICULTY	♿
1,000 feet	7,400 feet	♦ ♦ ♦	No

TRAIL ACCESSIBLE		
Jan Feb Mar Apr May Jun **Jul Aug Sep Oct** Nov Dec		

The Hike

One of the most spectacular alpine day hikes from Sunrise, the Burroughs Mountain Trail is a fairly strenuous climb along the top of Burroughs Mountain in a bizarre, tundra-like environment with incredible views throughout.

Getting There

From the park's White River Entrance on Highway 410, proceed 14 miles to Sunrise, elevation 6,400 feet. Begin to the right of the restrooms and walk to the trail's start at the picnic area. Follow signs to the left (west) toward Frozen Lake.

The Trail

Like many other city-sized chunks of rock around here, Burroughs is a fascinating geologic oddity. It's actually part of an old lava flow, left exposed after softer earth was eroded away on either side. As such,

PERMITS/CONTACT
Entrance fee; no day-hiking passes required/
Sunrise Visitor Center, (360) 663-2425

MAPS
Green Trails No. 270, Mount Rainier East; USGS Sunrise

TRAIL NOTES
No dogs; no bikes

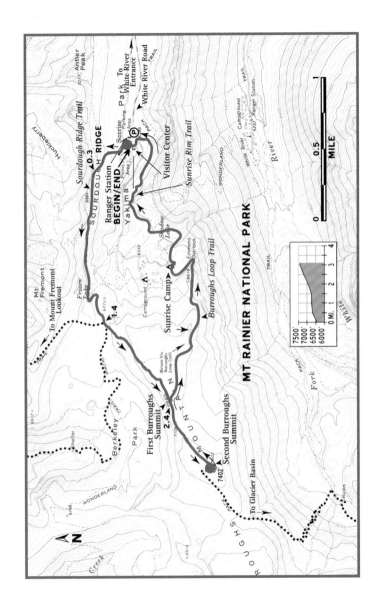

N

Antler Peak 7076

To White River Entrance

White River Road

Park

TRAIL

Huckleberry

Sourdough Ridge Trail

0.3

SOURDOUGH RIDGE

Sunrise Parking Area

Ranger Station

BEGIN/END

Picnic Area

Yakima

Visitor Center

Sunrise Rim Trail

Mt. Fremont

To Mount Fremont Lookout

6884

Shadow Lake

6232

Frozen

6772

1.4

Campground

Emmons Overlook

6615

Sunrise Camp

WONDERLAND

TRAIL

4400

White River Campground 4232 Ranger Station

4400

4600

River

MT RAINIER NATIONAL PARK

Burroughs Loop Trail

4600

4600

Berkeley TRAIL

Shelter

8947

Park

TRAIL

MOUNTAIN

(Return Via Burroughs Loop Trail)

2.4

First Burroughs Summit

Second Burroughs Summit

7402

PACK

Fork

White

WONDERLAND

6788

B U R R O U G H S

To Glacier Basin

6919

Creek

PACK

TRAIL

6916

0   0.5   1
MILE

7500'
7000'
6500'
6000'
0 Mi.   1   2   3   4

The terrain on the Burroughs Mountain Loop is rocky, barren, and stunning

and given its high altitude, the upper mountain supports only tiny vegetation growth; stay on the trail, for your own safety and that of the plants, which take years to grow back after you trample them.

Burroughs can be approached from either of two ways: via the Sourdough Ridge and Frozen Lake route described here, or by hiking the Sunrise Rim Trail toward Sunrise Camp (Hike 37) and approaching Burroughs's ridgeline from the southeast via the Burroughs Loop Trail. To add variety to your hike, consider going up in one direction and coming down the other: Making this quasi loop adds only about 0.5 mile to the overall distance.

We prefer the Frozen Lake approach, however, primarily for its dramatic, in-your-face view of Rainier's summit as you climb the Burroughs Mountain ridgeline. To get there, walk the Sourdough Ridge Trail from Sunrise up the ridge and to the left, toward Frozen Lake (Hike 40). At the five-way trail junction near Frozen Lake (1.4 miles,

6,785 feet), stay left where signs point up the hill, southwest, to Burroughs Mountain.

The trail ascends a steady mile. Views dead ahead are of Rainier's summit—particularly beautiful as it falls under ghostly shadows in late afternoon. Below to the north is the great, flat, green (or bronze, in early fall) plateau of the Berkeley Park area—a shocking contrast to the sheer, rocky vertical terrain you're crossing. Watch for marmots on the uphill slopes here. One major safety caveat: This stretch of trail crosses a steep, extremely hazardous snowfield that often lingers well into August, and in some years never fully melts out. Do not attempt to cross it without lug-soled boots and an ice ax or other means to self-arrest. A tiny slip here can be—and has been—deadly.

The trail finally flattens out at the top of First Burroughs at **2.4** miles and about 7,100 feet. Just short of the summit is a junction with the Burroughs Loop Trail, descending to the Sunrise Rim Trail. Stay straight, drop a short way, and then climb again 0.75 mile to Second Burroughs summit, elevation 7,402 feet. On a clear day, grander alpine vistas are tough to find anywhere on Planet Earth. As you face Rainier, the summit, Little Tahoma Peak, and the massive Emmons (left) and Winthrop (right) Glaciers all look close enough to touch. Tiny wildflowers and blooming sprigs of heather are found here in late summer.

Going Farther

The path drops from here another 1.4 miles—and a toe-blackening 1,900 feet—to Glacier Basin and an exit at White River Campground (Hike 34). Save that for another lifetime. Turn around and retrace your steps through the moonscape back to First Burroughs and a right-hand (east) turn down the Burroughs Loop Trail. It's about 3.0 miles back to Sunrise this way via Sunrise Camp, Shadow Lake, and the Sunrise Rim Trail (Hike 37). If you go this way, note that another steep snowfield, which also usually lingers into late summer, must be crossed about 0.5 mile above Sunrise Camp. Use extreme caution.

Note: Carry plenty of water—it's scarce along the route. ■

42. Berkeley Park

RATING	DISTANCE	HIKING TIME
★★★	7.8 miles round-trip	4.0 hours
ELEVATION GAIN	**HIGH POINT**	**DIFFICULTY** ♿
1,600 feet	6,773 feet	♦ ♦ ◇ ◇ ◇ No

TRAIL ACCESSIBLE
Jan Feb Mar Apr May Jun **Jul Aug Sep Oct** Nov Dec

The Hike

The walk to Berkeley Park takes you first up, and then down through alpine tundra to a wide meadow filled with just about every wildflower to be found around Mount Rainier.

Getting There

From the park's White River Entrance on Highway 410, proceed 14 miles to Sunrise, elevation 6,400 feet. The trailhead begins on the north side of the parking lot at the paved access to the Sourdough Ridge Trail.

The Trail

Sunrise gets mighty crowded in the late summer, but the meadows of Berkeley Park might not be visited as frequently simply because day hikers have so many trails from which to choose. Since the walk to Berkeley involves one steady, 800-foot climb—and a total ascent of 1,200 feet—on the way home, fewer hikers might choose it as their destination.

PERMITS/CONTACT
Entrance fee; no day-hiking passes required/
Sunrise Visitor Center, (360) 663-2425

MAPS
Green Trails No. 270, Mount Rainier East; USGS Sunrise

TRAIL NOTES
No dogs; kid-friendly; no bikes

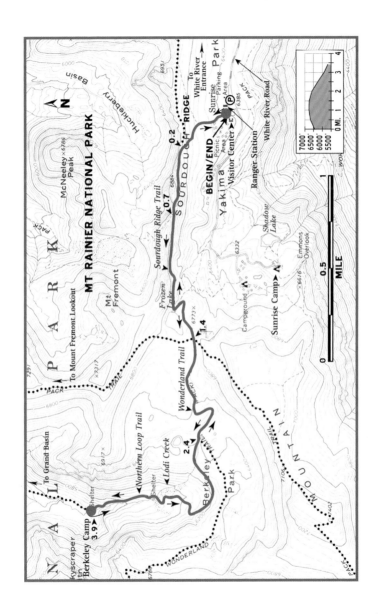

The path to Berkeley Park often provides the rare commodity of solitude

Regardless, there's plenty of views and wildflower watching to share with everyone you encounter. Begin by climbing from the trailhead to a junction with the Sourdough Ridge Trail, 0.1 mile from the parking area. Keep left at the junction and climb briefly to a junction with the Huckleberry Creek Trail. Stay left here and continue along Sourdough Ridge to the five-way trail junction near Frozen Lake, 1.4 miles from the trailhead, and the high point for this hike.

Hey: Flip a coin. Do you think a guidebook should give you every answer? Okay, follow the Wonderland Trail as it goes west from the junction beyond Frozen Lake and begins to descend gently under the cliffs of Burroughs Mountain (Hike 41). Crumbled parts of the mountain decorate the hillside on your left as you descend and pikas cry "knee!" from their rock thrones.

The trail continues to drop into a wide, flat meadow to a junction with the Northern Loop Trail at **2.4** miles. Turn right on the Northern Loop Trail and follow it as it descends more steeply into Berkeley Park, the valley formed by Lodi Creek. Above the flower-filled valley is Mount Fremont, on the right, and Skyscraper Mountain on the left. The trail winds through the valley for about a mile before entering the subalpine forest and coming to Berkeley Camp at **3.9** miles. This is the turnaround point for day hikers, and a good spot for those who carry filter pumps or bottles to replenish their water supply.

Going Farther

Strong hikers who don't mind climbing 1,500 vertical feet back to the trailhead should consider continuing past Berkeley Camp for another 3 miles to Grand Park, a mile-long meadow flat as a pancake griddle. The return trip affords a splendid view of Mount Rainier. The trail first climbs, and then descends past the camp, leveling off and striking the Lake Eleanor Trail junction at 6.9 miles. Follow the Lake Eleanor Trail to the right into Grand Park. When you reach the place where a 747 might land safely, turn around and check out the view of Rainier. ■

43. Skyscraper Pass

RATING	DISTANCE	HIKING TIME	
★ ★ ★	7.2 miles round-trip	3.5 hours	
ELEVATION GAIN	HIGH POINT	DIFFICULTY	♿
1,300 feet	6,773 feet	♦ ♦	No
	TRAIL ACCESSIBLE		
	Jul Aug Sep Oct		

The Hike

Wander up and down—then up—through flowery meadows to an airy view of The Mountain that you may well enjoy with company of the mountain goat kind.

Getting There

From the park's White River Entrance on Highway 410, proceed 14 miles to Sunrise, elevation 6,400 feet. The trailhead begins on the north side of the parking lot at the paved access to the Sourdough Ridge Trail.

A hiker on the Wonderland Trail, with Rainier's summit in the distance

The Trail

The hike to Skyscraper Pass might be another trail many of the hikers at Sunrise avoid, simply because it involves a moderate climb on the return trip. Views from the pass and the chance to picnic with some of the local wildlife might make the hike worth the effort. You'll share the trail with hikers bound for Mount Fremont for the first

PERMITS/CONTACT
Entrance fee; no day-hiking passes required/
White River Wilderness Information Center, (360) 569-6670

MAPS
Green Trails No. 270, Mount Rainier East; USGS Sunrise

TRAIL NOTES
No dogs; kid-friendly; no bikes

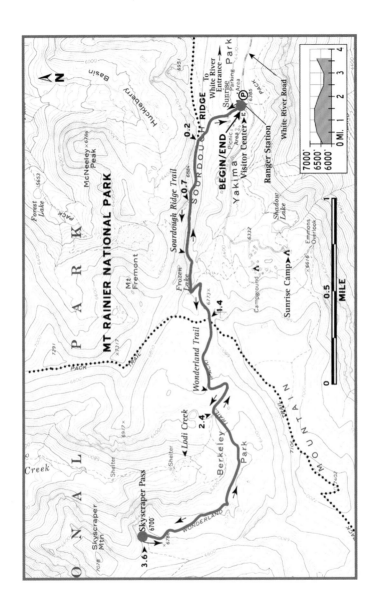

N

Huckleberry
Basin

MT RAINIER NATIONAL PARK

McNeeley × 6769
Peak

Forest
Lake
5653

PACK

P A R K

Mt
Fremont
7317×

7291

PACK
6800

6947 ×

Sourdough Ridge Trail

6894

Frozen
Lake

6773×

0.2

0.7

1.4

Wonderland Trail

SOURDOUGH RIDGE

To
White River
Entrance →

Sunrise
Parking
Area

PACK

P
6305

BEGIN/END

Yakima
Picnic
Area

Sunrise
Visitor Center

Ranger Station

White River Road

Shadow
Lake

6332

Campground

Sunrise Camp▲

6919×

Emmons
Overlook

O N A L

Skyscraper
Mtn
7078

Creek

Shelter
7085

Lodi Creek

2.4

Berkeley
Park

Shelter

Skyscraper Pass
6700

3.6

6789×

WONDERLAND

4600

5600

5600

6000

M O U N T A I N
PACK

7000'
6500'
6000'

0 MI. 1 2 3 4

0   0.5   1
MILE

1.4 miles and with Berkeley Park–bound hikers for another mile, until you swing off on the Wonderland Trail to the pass, a high saddle underneath Skyscraper Mountain.

The first portion of the trail is on the same route you may (or may not) have already hiked on Hikes 39–42: from the Sunrise parking area, 0.3 mile up the Sourdough Ridge Trail to the ridge top above Sunrise Camp, proceeding west to a five-way junction at Frozen Lake, 1.4 miles. Stay left on the Wonderland Trail, which heads west beyond Frozen Lake and begins a gentle descent under the rocky flank of Burroughs Mountain.

The trail drops through two flat meadowland benches, reaching a junction with the Northern Loop Trail at **2.4** miles. Turn left at this junction, climb over a knoll, and begin a long ascending traverse to Skyscraper Pass, 3.6 miles from the trailhead. The climb to the pass is on a moderate grade, but may seem steeper on a dry, hot day. In the autumn, the upper tributaries to Lodi Creek may be dry, so plan to bring plenty of water with you.

The pass, at 6,700 feet, is at about the same elevation as Frozen Lake. Granite Creek tumbles from the Winthrop Glacier and Sluiskin Mountain guards the valley to the west. ■

CARBON GLACIER/ MOWICH LAKE

Please note, some of these trails may have been affected by recent weather patterns and repairs may be underway. Always call ahead to guarantee trail accessibility.

44. Green Lake

RATING ★★★	DISTANCE 6.0 mile round-trip to trailhead; 3.6 mile round-trip hike	HIKING TIME 2.0 hours (trail only)	
ELEVATION GAIN 1,120 feet	HIGH POINT 3,220 feet	DIFFICULTY ◆◆	♿ Yes (FROM CARBON RIVER ROAD TO LAKE TURNOFF)
TRAIL ACCESSIBLE Jan Feb Mar Apr May Jun **Jul Aug Sep Oct** Nov Dec			

The Hike

Enjoy a great family hike past spectacular Ranger Falls to a quiet (in the autumn) lake surrounded by an avalanche-swept hillside and forest.

Getting There

From Puyallup, follow Highway 410 about 13 miles east to Buckley. Turn right (south) onto Highway 165, crossing the bridge over the Carbon River. Bear left to the Mount Rainier National Park Carbon River entrance. Walk or bicycle 3 miles up the Carbon River Road to the trailhead on the left.

The Trail

Note: This is one of many day hikes in this section of the book in the Carbon River drainage that have become very long day hikes or

PERMITS/CONTACT
Entrance fee; no day-hiking passes required/
Carbon River Ranger Station,(360) 829-9639

MAPS
Green Trails No. 269, Mount Rainier West; USGS Carbon River

TRAIL NOTES
No dogs; kid-friendly; no bikes

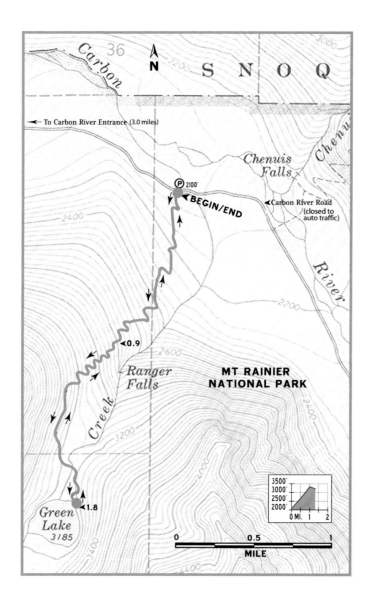

To Carbon River Entrance (3.0 miles)

(P) 2100'

BEGIN/END

Chenuis Falls

Carbon River Road (closed to auto traffic)

0.9

Ranger Falls

MT RAINIER NATIONAL PARK

1.8

Green Lake 3185

3500'
3000'
2500'
2000'
0 MI.   1   2

0   0.5   1
MILE

Three guesses as to the color of your destination lake

bike/hikes because of the now-permanent closure to automobiles of the washed-out Carbon River Road at the park entrance.

This is a popular hike in the late spring and summer, often yielding (forgive us) sole-to-soul hiking. So wait until mid-September, when you will share the trail with fewer people and perhaps more elk. For maximum solitude and a better chance at seeing wildlife, plan this walk in the early morning or evening.

The youngsters will flat-out love this hike, not only for the shallow, log-walking lakeshore at the destination, but for the wide number of diversions along the way. A cattle prod might come in handy to keep the kids moving, especially when they spot the three fallen Really Big Trees that bridge the trail.

After making the 3-mile trek to the trailhead by foot or bike, you'll wander the forest flats beside Ranger Creek for about 0.1 mile before beginning to climb in switchbacks alongside the creek. The trail tunnels underneath the first Really Big Tree, switches back to a second, and eventually climbs to a third tree that is likely too high and too far off the trail to beckon young climbers.

At about **0.7** mile, you'll find a way trail at one switchback leading to low cascading falls that some hikers might mistake for Ranger Falls. Nope; you must continue climbing for another 0.2 mile to another switchback and signed trail leading 100 yards to the left to a fenced overlook of the much higher and more spectacular Ranger Falls.

Back on the trail, you'll continue climbing in switchbacks another quarter mile, and then traverse along the hillside to a footlog crossing of Ranger Creek at **1.5** miles. Cross the creek, which is wide and still, and climb to the high point of the hike, 3,220 feet, before dropping steeply down to Green Lake's north shore.

The maintained trail ends at the lakeshore, 1.8 miles from the trailhead. Log hoppers can follow the shoreline west to the mouth of the outlet and the open shoreline to the southwest. ■

45. Really Big Tree/Ipsut Pass

RATING ★★☆☆☆	DISTANCE 10.0 mile round-trip to trailhead; 6.4 mile round-trip hike	HIKING TIME 4.0 hours (trail only)	
ELEVATION GAIN 2,800 feet	HIGH POINT 5,100 feet	DIFFICULTY ◆◆◆◇	👨‍🦽 No
	TRAIL ACCESSIBLE Jan Feb Mar Apr May Jun **Jul Aug Sep Oct** Nov Dec		

The Hike
Make a strenuous climb through a forest of really big trees to a conifer said to be the world's largest Alaska Cedar—a real Really Big Tree.

Getting There
From Puyallup, follow Highway 410 about 13 miles east to Buckley. Turn right (south) onto Highway 165, crossing the bridge over the Carbon River. Bear left to the Mount Rainier National Park Carbon River entrance. Walk or bicycle 5 miles up the Carbon River Road to the trailhead at the former Ipsut Creek Campground, elevation 2,300 feet.

The Trail
The world's largest Alaska cedar grows right smack dab beside the trail to Ipsut Pass, which could come as something of a surprise to the

Falls along the Ipsut Creek Trail to the Really Big Tree

good people of Olympic National Park, who claim that the world's largest Alaska cedar is on the Big Creek Trail in the Quinault River valley. Superintendents from each park need to duke it out to determine the champion tree. Nonetheless, if you enjoy looking at big trees, this is a hike for you.

Getting here, of course, is a bit tougher than it used to be. But those willing to walk or mountain bike 5 miles to the trailhead are in for a treat, and probably fewer people than when the Carbon River Road remained open to traffic. On the main trail, you'll first pass by a large Douglas fir whose nurse log long ago turned to forest duff,

PERMITS/CONTACT
Entrance fee; no day-hiking passes required/
Carbon River Ranger Station, (360) 569-6624

MAPS
Green Trails No. 269, Mount Rainier West; USGS Golden Lakes

TRAIL NOTES
No dogs; kid-friendly; no bikes

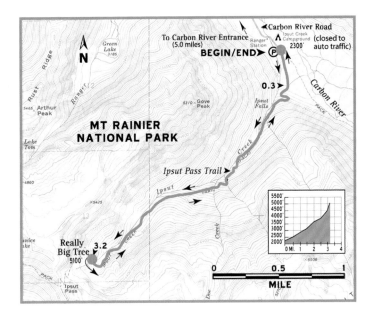

leaving a cave underneath the tree suitable for hobbits and children alike. The warren even has a window and back door. Shortly after passing the really big fir, you'll encounter a huge western red cedar. Your aching muscles may at this point try to convince you that this is the genuine Really Big Tree. It is not. You must climb farther.

But first things first: Begin the hike by following the Carbon River Trail from the parking lot, passing the side trail to Ipsut Falls in 0.1 mile. Begin a traversing climb that ends at **0.3** mile from the parking lot at a junction with the Ipsut Pass Trail. Turn right here and begin the serious climbing up the ridge above Ipsut Creek on the right. The trail wastes little time gaining elevation, climbing with few switchbacks through an ancient forest, which serves up a blueberry feast in early fall.

You'll find the Douglas fir hobbit house about 1.2 miles from the trailhead, a good turnaround point for families with younger children. The trail continues climbing—more steeply now—and passes the huge red cedar at about **1.4** miles. After switching back once, you'll cross a creek on a footlog and climb to a second creek where a footbridge affords a great spot to get a photo of the splendid cascade on your left. This is the kind of waterfall you'd bring home to meet the parents, although doing so would likely cause substantial grousing from the Department of the Interior.

Now the trail climbs along the crest of a low ridge that divides two branches of Ipsut Creek. Huge conifers provide a hallway through the forest. As the low ridge rises steeply in front of you, you'll begin traversing upward along the right side. The forest thins and trees grow smaller as the valley below opens into an alpine meadow, 2.8 miles from the trailhead.

You leave the forest behind at **3.0** miles and the character of the trail turns from smooth dirt to alpine rock immediately. You'll cross a stream and wet meadow and climb steeply to a grove of Alaska cedars, directly ahead. The trail passes between two really big Alaska cedars on the right and three really big Alaska cedars uphill on the left.

It is difficult to tell which of the trees is largest, but one is the Really Big Tree. It appears that the biggest cedar on the right had a top broken off from an avalanche and the tallest cedar is now the middle one on the left. No sign marked the world record tree on our last visit here. But it doesn't matter. None are as large as some of the really big conifers you've seen down the trail. If it is sunny, enjoy the shade these trees give. If it is raining, enjoy their shelter. It's time for a picnic before heading back down.

Going Farther

You can continue up the trail another very steep 0.8 mile, switching back under cliffs to Ipsut Pass, where the trail joins the path to Eunice Lake and Tolmie Peak that comes from Mowich Lake. Other than more exercise, though, there's little point in climbing past the Really Big Tree since you can hike to Ipsut Pass by following the much easier Tolmie Peak Trail 1.5 miles from Mowich Lake (Hike 50). ■

46. Carbon Glacier Viewpoint

RATING	DISTANCE	HIKING TIME
★★★★	10.0 mile round-trip to trailhead; 7.0 mile round-trip hike	3.5 hours (trail only)

ELEVATION GAIN	HIGH POINT	DIFFICULTY	⚐
1,200 feet	3,400 feet	♦♦◇◇◇	No

TRAIL ACCESSIBLE
Jan Feb Mar Apr May Jun **Jul Aug Sep Oct** Nov Dec

Note: Footlogs on this trail at various stream crossings are particularly prone to winter washouts. Check trail conditions on the park website, or with rangers, particularly if you are hiking this trail in the early summer, before trail crews have worked their magic.

The Hike
Once one of the easiest ways in Mount Rainier National Park to get up close and personal with a real, live glacier, the trek to the snout of Carbon Glacier is now long because of road closures. It's still worth the trek for hardier hoofers.

Getting There
From Puyallup, follow Highway 410 about 13 miles east to Buckley. Turn right (south) onto Highway 165, crossing the bridge over the Carbon River. Bear left to the Mount Rainier National Park Carbon

PERMITS/CONTACT
Entrance fee; no day-hiking passes required/
Carbon River Ranger Station, (360) 569-6624

MAPS
Green Trails No. 269, Mount Rainier West; USGS Carbon River

TRAIL NOTES
No dogs; kid-friendly; no bikes

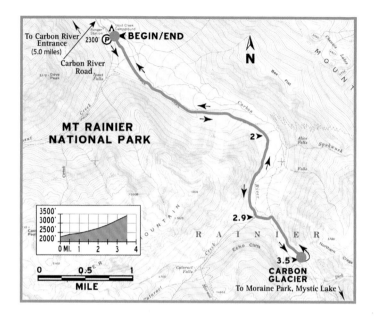

To Carbon River Entrance (5.0 miles)

Ranger Station
Ipsut Creek Campground
2300' **BEGIN/END**

Carbon River Road

MT RAINIER NATIONAL PARK

N

2▶

2.9▶

3.5▶
CARBON GLACIER
To Moraine Park, Mystic Lake

3500'
3000'
2500'
2000'

0 MI. 1 2 3 4

0 0.5 1
MILE

R A I N I E R

River entrance. Walk or bicycle 5 miles up the Carbon River Road to the trailhead at the former Ipsut Creek Campground, elevation 2,300 feet.

The Trail

The hike to the snout of the Carbon Glacier follows a long-abandoned roadbed and the trail is seldom more than hearing distance away from the silty Carbon River. Once you make it up those long 5 miles on the Carbon River Road to the trailhead (see page 169), the river is fewer than 3 miles from where it gushes from beneath the glacier.

Begin by following the Carbon River Trail in glacier-ground sand through the forest for 0.1 mile to a junction with a side trail to Ipsut Falls. Stay left at the junction and begin a moderate climb through forest that ends 0.2 mile from the trailhead at a junction with the Ipsut Pass Trail. Stay left at this junction as the trail continues to climb more gently through the forest above the river. The trail turns toward the river and rejoins the old roadbed above the watercourse, where the rushing river tumbles boulders clunking downstream.

As the trail rounds a ridge, hikers can get their first view of the glacier, still 1.5 miles upstream. The trail eventually enters the forest and begins to climb away from the main course of the river underneath cliffs and broken shards of the ridge above. At **2.0** miles from the trailhead, you'll find a junction with the Northern Loop Trail. Stay right and continue to climb gently past Carbon River Camp at **2.8** miles.

Past the camp, the trail drops to a footlog crossing Cataract Creek, just below one of the low falls that gave the creek its name. On the far side of the creek, you'll find a junction with the Seattle Park Trail. Stay left here, and climb a short hill to a suspension bridge over the Carbon River, 3.0 miles from the trailhead. The suspension bridge is a great thrill to cross. It's high above the river and sways and bounces slightly as hikers navigate the planks. You'll see the dirty snout of the glacier upstream from the bridge. In the fall, the tread from the bridge is sometimes removed to avoid damage by heavy winter snows; if the bridge is closed, a well-marked trail leads to footlogs across the river.

Once across the river, turn right on the trail and follow it as it begins to climb steeply under glacier-polished cliffs beside the river of ice. This is the steepest part of the trail, and it reaches a viewpoint of the glacier's frozen leading wave at **3.5** miles from the trailhead.

The snout of the Carbon Glacier hides beneath moraine debris

Pick out a big trailside rock seat and watch the Carbon River being born. A sign warns hikers about straying too close to the ice, which could crack into chunks definitely too large for your margarita, or spill rocks it carries from above.

Going Farther

Although the glacier viewpoint might be the best turnaround spot for many wilderness pedestrians, the 2,000-foot climb up past Dick Creek Camp to Moraine Park, 6.6 miles from the trailhead, yields splendid views of The Mountain and a spectacular alpine meadow. Strong hikers may choose to continue through Moraine Park to Mystic Lake, a beautiful alpine lake nestled under the north face of Rainier, 7.5 miles from the trailhead. ∎

47. Cataract Camp/Seattle Park

RATING	DISTANCE	HIKING TIME
★★☆☆☆	10.0 mile round-trip to trailhead; 8.4 mile round-trip hike	5.5 hours (trail only)

ELEVATION GAIN	HIGH POINT	DIFFICULTY	♿
2,400 feet	4,700 feet	♦♦♦♦	No

TRAIL ACCESSIBLE											
Jan	Feb	Mar	Apr	May	Jun	**Jul**	**Aug**	**Sep**	**Oct**	Nov	Dec

The Hike

Climb into an open valley so thick with blueberries you can't return without purple mouth and hands. You'll be surrounded by high cliffs with a wide view of the dark forests of the Carbon River on the way home. Strong hikers can climb another 500 feet and 1.5 miles into beautiful Seattle Park underneath Echo Rock and the Russell Glacier.

Getting There

From Puyallup, follow Highway 410 about 13 miles east to Buckley. Turn right (south) onto Highway 165, crossing the bridge over the

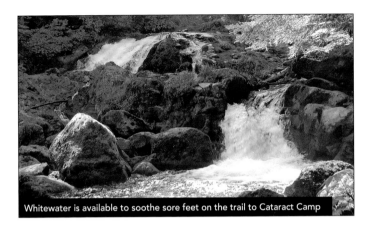
Whitewater is available to soothe sore feet on the trail to Cataract Camp

Carbon River. Bear left to the Mount Rainier National Park Carbon River entrance. Walk or bicycle 5 miles up the Carbon River Road to the trailhead at the former Ipsut Creek Campground, elevation 2,300 feet.

The Trail

Hikers in search of solitude are likely to find more of it on this trail than on most others around the Carbon River, since it is a long, hard climb past Cataract Camp into the open alpine country of Seattle Park. This is especially true given the added burden of walking or cycling 5 miles up the former Carbon River Road just to get to the trailhead (see page 169). Begin by following the Carbon River Trail past its junction with a spur trail leading right to Ipsut Falls, at **0.1** mile, and uphill to a junction at **0.3** mile with the

---

PERMITS/CONTACT
Entrance fee; no day-hiking passes required/
Carbon River Ranger Station, (360) 569-6624

MAPS
Green Trails No. 269, Mount Rainier West; USGS Golden Lakes

TRAIL NOTES
No dogs ; no bikes

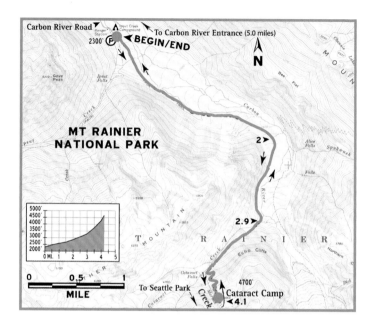

Ipsut Pass Trail. Stay left at this junction and continue along the abandoned road as it alternately winds through forest and beside the silty, raging Carbon River.

At **2.0** miles, you'll strike a junction with the Northern Loop Trail. Stay right at the junction and in another 0.8 mile, pass Carbon River Camp. Drop to a footlog crossing of Cataract Creek where, if you look upstream, you'll get a pretty good idea of how the creek was named. Cross the footlog to find the junction with the trail climbing to Seattle and Spray Parks. Turn right here and begin the serious climbing to Cataract Camp.

The first half mile of this trail climbs in steep switchbacks where the highbush blueberries lining the trail in the fall are likely to slow your pace far more than the grade. The grade lessens somewhat in the next half mile, but the berries do not.

About 3.6 miles from the trailhead, the view up the valley opens to show cliffs of Mother Mountain. The trail switches back and continues to climb above Marmot Creek before arriving at Cataract Camp, 4.2 miles from the trailhead.

The camp makes a good picnic spot and turnaround for most day hikers. If you've been grazing on berries, perhaps you can save your lunch for another hike.

Going Farther

Hikers looking for more spectacular views and beautiful alpine meadows can continue to climb another 500 feet and 1.5 miles to the lower edge of Seattle Park. From there, the trail continues to climb another 1,200 feet and 1.5 miles to the ridge that divides Seattle Park from Spray Park—but hikers headed there will have a much easier go of it by taking the trail from Mowich Lake (Hike 51). ■

48. Yellowstone Cliffs

RATING	DISTANCE	HIKING TIME
★☆☆☆☆	10.0 mile round-trip to trailhead; 10.2 mile round-trip hike	6.0 hours (trail only)
ELEVATION GAIN	**HIGH POINT**	**DIFFICULTY** ♿
2,800 feet	5,100 feet	♦♦♦♦ No
TRAIL ACCESSIBLE		
~~Jan~~ ~~Feb~~ ~~Mar~~ ~~Apr~~ ~~May~~ ~~Jun~~ Jul Aug Sep Oct ~~Nov~~ ~~Dec~~		

The Hike

This is a marvelous workout for wilderness pedestrians in search of an excuse to gobble ibuprofen or to count switchbacks. You'll climb to a good view of some really big rock columns in wide alpine meadows.

Getting There

From Puyallup, follow Highway 410 about 13 miles east to Buckley. Turn right (south) onto Highway 165, crossing the bridge over the

Carbon River. Bear left to the Mount Rainier National Park Carbon River entrance. Walk or bicycle 5 miles up the Carbon River Road to the trailhead (see page 169) at the former Ipsut Creek Campground, elevation 2,300 feet.

The Trail

Masochistic hikers will be disappointed in the first couple of miles of this trail, because it is relatively easy walking. Sadistic hikers should take their only comfort in this section, knowing the masochists aren't suffering nearly enough. Both groups should be happy now that the closure of the Carbon River Road at the park boundary has turned this previously tough day hike into a seriously tough trek—one that, candidly, pushes the definition of "day hike" for most hikers.

The trail follows an abandoned road alongside the Carbon River for 2 miles, passing a junction with the Ipsut Falls Trail at **0.1** mile and with the Ipsut Pass Trail at **0.3** mile. Stay left at both these junctions. The trail climbs through forest, under cliffs, and beside the boulder-strewn path of the Carbon River to a junction with the Northern Loop Trail, 2.0 miles from the trailhead. Turn left onto it and descend to the valley floor.

The path winds through the forest and crosses two footlogs to the boulder field shaped by the river. In the fall, the Carbon is usually low and a footlog crossing has been constructed across the pewter ribbons of water. The footlogs, however, are frequently washed out in spring and summer and hikers not wishing to risk fording must continue

PERMITS/CONTACT
Entrance fee; no day-hiking passes required/
Carbon River Ranger Station, (360) 569-6624

MAPS
Green Trails No. 269, Mount Rainier West; USGS Carbon River and Sunrise

TRAIL NOTES
No dogs; no bikes

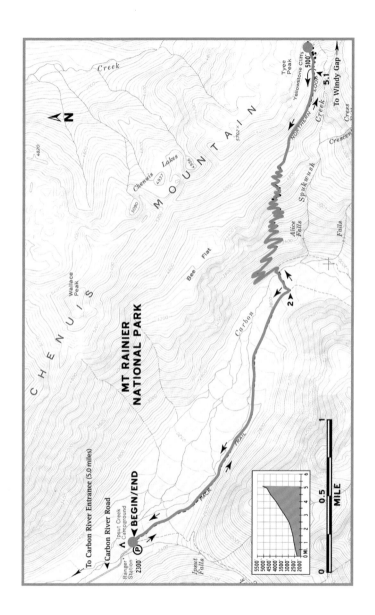

another mile upstream to the suspension bridge crossing, and then follow the trail downstream on the other side to the Northern Loop Trail.

Once across the footlog, the trail meanders downstream several hundred yards before beginning its steep climb. It gains more than 2,000 vertical feet in the next 3 miles, following thirty-six switchbacks on a steady grade. The path is through the forest, which provides shade and on an autumn day may makes the way seem less steep. The trail never ceases climbing, even when it reaches the junction with the Yellowstone Cliff Camp Trail, 5.1 miles from the trailhead. Here you'll find the first of the alpine meadows, a view of the rock columns of Yellowstone Cliffs, and a good spot beside the trail where—it you are

The route to Yellowstone Cliffs crosses the Carbon River a few miles below the snout of the Carbon Glacier

in as good a physical condition as us—you'll flop like an exhausted flounder to the ground, begging for someone to shoot you.

Going Farther

Though it never would cross our minds that any sane hiker would want to continue this painful journey, you can climb another 0.5 mile (and 500 vertical feet) to Windy Gap. It may live up to its name on some days, but on calm autumn afternoons, its meadows make a fine place to wonder why in the world anyone would want to work so hard to get here. ■

49. Mowich River Camp

RATING	DISTANCE	HIKING TIME	
★★★★	7.2 miles round-trip	4.0 hours	
ELEVATION GAIN	HIGH POINT	DIFFICULTY	♿
2,860 feet	4,200 feet	♦♦♦	No
TRAIL ACCESSIBLE			
Jan Feb Mar Apr May Jun **Jul Aug Sep Oct** Nov Dec			

The Hike

This walk is mostly downhill on the way to Mowich River Camp, but the climb back to the trailhead may seem easier because the excellent path is so nicely graded. It's a good hike for a foggy or rainy day.

Getting There

From Wilkeson, follow Highway 165 south for 9 miles to a junction with the Carbon River Road. Continue right (south) on the highway, and proceed about 12 miles to the Paul Peak trailhead on the right (south) side of the road, elevation 3,700 feet. You'll find an unmanned fee station at the parking area, where you can pay the park entrance fee if you don't have an annual pass.

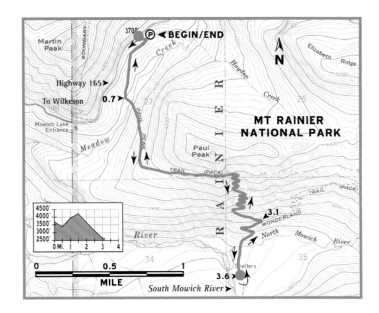

The Trail

Although the peekaboo shots through the forest of the North Mowich Glacier are impressive, this hike is mostly short on views. For that reason alone, you might choose a less than perfect day for this walk.

But here are a couple of other good reasons for adding this trek to your list of must-dos: The trail is so consistently graded that you'll barely realize you are climbing and dropping more than 2,800 ver-

PERMITS/CONTACT
Entrance fee; no day-hiking passes required/
Carbon River Ranger Station, (360) 569-6624

MAPS
Green Trails No. 269, Mount Rainier West; USGS Golden Lakes

TRAIL NOTES
No dogs; kid-friendly; no bikes

tical feet on the walk down and back. You might also have a better chance of spotting wildlife along this trail, both in the wide flats around Meadow Creek and on the rich bottomland at the confluence of the north and south forks of the Mowich River.

The hike begins with the steepest hill first, a 0.7-mile section down—which by no strange coincidence is up on the way home. You'll drop into the head of the flat green valley of Meadow Creek, probably the best turnaround point for families with small children. You can explore upstream from the footbridge crossing the creek to the meadows that give the creek its name. Across the creek, the trail now begins a gently graded 1.5-mile climb around the shoulder of Paul Peak. This part of the route traverses through splendid old forest on a smooth, wide trail.

As the hillside steepens, you'll approach a dry gully dropping down to the North Mowich River. The trail switches back seventeen times— down more than 1,600 vertical feet—but the grade is so consistent that you can often see two or three switchbacks ahead. Please cut them only with your eyes. At **3.1** miles, you'll strike the junction with

The Mowich Camp shelter makes a good rainy-day destination on the Paul Peak Trail

the Wonderland Trail. Turn right here, onto the Wonderland Trail, and drop the final switchbacks down to a footlog crossing of the river.

You'll cross a second branch on a footlog, and then wander through forested bottomland to the South Mowich River, where you'll find a shelter, campsites, and your turnaround point, 3.6 miles from the trailhead. ■

50. Tolmie Peak/Eunice Lake

RATING	DISTANCE	HIKING TIME
★★★	6.2 miles round-trip	3.5 hours

ELEVATION GAIN	HIGH POINT	DIFFICULTY	♿
1,120 feet	5,939 feet	♦♦♦♦	No

TRAIL ACCESSIBLE
Jan Feb Mar Apr May Jun **Jul Aug Sep Oct** Nov Dec

The Hike
This walk to beautiful alpine meadows around a clear alpine lake, followed by a tough climb to an old fire lookout, could be one of the finest hikes in the park, except for the part of the foot-worn trail in horrid condition.

PERMITS/CONTACT
Entrance fee; no day-hiking passes required/
Carbon River Ranger Station, (360) 569-6624

MAPS
Green Trails No. 269, Mount Rainier West; USGS Carbon River

TRAIL NOTES
Not a good choice for kids

Eunice Lake lies below the Tolmie Peak Lookout

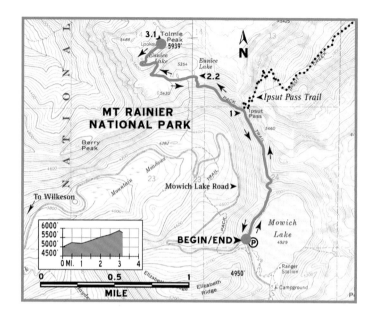

Getting There

From Wilkeson, follow Highway 165 south for 9 miles to a junction with the Carbon River Road. Continue right (south) on the highway, and proceed about 12 miles to the Paul Peak trailhead on the right (south) side of the road, elevation 3,700 feet. You'll find an unmanned fee station at the parking area where you can pay the park entrance fee if you don't have an annual pass. Continue another 5.3 miles to the Mowich Lake parking area. The Tolmie Peak trailhead, elevation 4,950 feet, is located at the west end of the lake on the left, just as the road flattens above the lake. Park along the north side of the road, or continue to the larger parking area at the east end of the lake and add about 0.6 mile round-trip to the hike.

The Trail

Your feet will tell you this trail is longer than it really is, the result of a 0.5-mile climb up to Eunice Lake that is more root and mud than trail. Though this trek is often recommended as a good hike for families with small children, your kids might have more fun if you took them to a big tar pit and threw them in.

But for that section of trail, this hike would earn a much higher rating. The meadows around Eunice Lake are a kaleidoscope of wild-flowers, the lake a spectacular mirror for Rainier, the Tolmie Peak lookout a fine spot from which to view the northeast side of Rainier and just about everything else in the galaxy. The hike begins with a walk along the west shoreline of Mowich Lake, with peekaboo views of Rainier and across the lake. The trail climbs in 0.2 mile to a low pass, switches back, and traverses through forest to the Ipsut Pass Trail junction, 1.0 mile from the trailhead.

You'll stay left at the junction, but for a good view of the Carbon River and Ipsut Creek valleys, follow the trail right a short way to Ipsut Pass. After that, the Ipsut Pass Trail drops very steeply in 0.8 mile to the Really Big Tree (Hike 45).

Back on the Tolmie Peak Trail, you'll traverse underneath cliffs on a gentle descent for about three-quarters of a mile to a wide, wet gully where the trail switchbacks up to the meadows around Eunice Lake. Here the path widens and wettens as hikers have attempted to circumnavigate slippery mud and roots, in some places carving little more than a wide dirt or mud road up the hillside. This portion of the trail is short, however, and is easily forgotten once you reach the meadows around Eunice Lake, 2.2 miles from the trailhead.

The lake is a good spot to picnic and turn around if you've brought the youngsters. For the 600-foot climb to the lookout, stay left at the Eunice Lake Trail junction and follow the path through meadows to the west end of the lake. The trail climbs in three switchbacks to a ridge and follows the ridge to the lookout, 3.1 miles from the trailhead. On a clear day, the view of Rainier, the surrounding foothills, and the lake below is one of the finest in the park. ■

51. Spray Park

RATING	DISTANCE	HIKING TIME	
★ ★ ★ ★ ★	6.0 miles round-trip	3.0–4.0 hours	
ELEVATION GAIN	HIGH POINT	DIFFICULTY	♿
2,200 feet	5,800 feet	♦ ♦ ◇ ◇ ◇	No
	TRAIL ACCESSIBLE		
	Jan Feb Mar Apr May Jun **Jul Aug Sep Oct** Nov Dec		

The Hike

One of Mount Rainier's premier—and most popular—wildflower hikes, Spray Park is a broad parkland reached by a moderately steep trail with a grand waterfall thrown in for good measure.

Getting There

From Wilkeson, follow Highway 165 south for 9 miles to a junction with the Carbon River Road. Continue right (south) on the highway, and proceed about 12 miles to the Paul Peak trailhead on the right (south) side of the road, elevation 3,700 feet. You'll find an unmanned fee station at the parking area where you can pay the park entrance fee if you don't have an annual pass. Continue another 5.3 miles to the Mowich Lake parking area, elevation 4,930 feet. Look for the well-signed Wonderland Trail trailhead near the lake at the south end of the parking lot.

PERMITS/CONTACT
Entrance fee; no day-hiking passes required/
Carbon River Ranger Station, (360) 569-6624

MAPS
Green Trails No. 269, Mount Rainier West; USGS Carbon River

TRAIL NOTES
No dogs; kid-friendly—for the older ones; no bikes

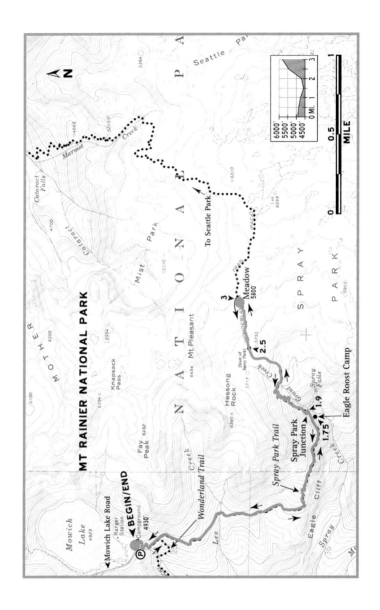

The Trail

There is no "there" here, which is just as well, because the splendor is, well, everywhere. That's our way of saying there's no official beginning or ending to Spray Park, the destination on this stellar hike. But you'll know it when you see the signs: a sprawling corridor of open meadows with unobstructed views of Mount Rainier and the North Mowich Glacier, dozens of sparkling tarns, squadrons of whistling marmots and—assuming you arrive in July and August along with most everyone else—acre after acre of splendiferous wildflowers.

The hike begins at Mowich Lake on the Wonderland Trail, beyond the restrooms and walk-in campground. Walk 0.25 mile downhill to a junction with the Spray Park Trail. Stay left, and you're off through the woods and on your way. The trail goes up and down in the first mile, south through a forest below Hessong Rock, before coming to a way trail at **1.5** miles. It leads a short distance to Eagle Cliff, a fine mountain viewpoint showcasing the North Mowich Glacier.

Skiers descend through Spray Park after a day on the Flett Glacier

After you've had a look, head up the main trail about another 0.2 mile, to another spur leading a short distance south to Eagle Roost Camp, the only backcountry campsite in this area. Just beyond Eagle Roost Camp is a short spur trail to Spray Falls. You can't see the entire falls from here, but it's a big one, and definitely worth the extra steps. Besides, you'll need a quick rest before the final climb back on the main trail, which switchbacks through the forest, now on a *very* steep grade toward Spray Park. Pace yourself: The trail is about 600 feet on nearly two dozen switchbacks over the final 0.5 mile to the meadows.

It's worth it, though. Soon, the trees will begin to fall away and the blue-sky spaces get larger. Before you know it, you're in the clear, entering Spray Park—a vast, rolling plain of tarns, rocky outcrops, and alpine greenery about 2.5 miles from the trailhead. If you hit it right, there may be no better wildflower treasure trove in the entire park, and perhaps on the entire planet. You can stop at the first meadows, but it's worth walking the extra 0.5 mile or so to the sprawling meadowland beneath 6,454-foot Mount Pleasant, to the north.

The parkland all around here begs to be explored by foot, but please keep in mind the damage your oversized lug soles do to fragile alpine meadows. Stay on established trails, find a good lunch spot, and soak up the splendor. Go as far as you like, but keep in mind that snow often lingers on the upper route well into August. The way is marked by cairns and wands, but don't venture too far if you're uncomfortable with, or ill-equipped for, snow travel.

Going Farther

If you proceed higher into the meadows, the trail tops out at a ridge at 6,400 feet, about 4 miles from the trailhead. Here, it begins its descent toward Seattle Park and the Carbon River drainage. Some strong hikers with a shuttle car used to like to hike beyond the high point another 2.6 miles north, through Seattle Park and past Cataract Camp to end at Ipsut Creek Campground (Hike 47) for a total through hike of about 11.5 miles. But you'll now have to add another 5 miles of hike/bike travel to get to that shuttle car, thanks to the closure of the Carbon River Road to auto traffic. ■

INDEX

ABOUT THE AUTHOR

Washington-state native **RON C. JUDD**, previously a veteran colum-nist and reporter at the *Seattle Times*, and now executive editor of *Cascadia Daily News*, has spent much of his life exploring the trails, campgrounds, streams, and beaches of the Pacific Northwest. The author of a half dozen best-selling guidebooks, two humor books, and a fan's guide to the Winter Olympics, he lives in Bellingham, Washington.